ENDORSE

Philip Renner has inspired me through his humility, passion, and love for God and people. The heart from which Philip worships and instructs on worship is one of purity, intimacy, and power. In contrast to some in this generation who lead from an egocentric or self-promoting place, Philip exemplifies what it means to glorify God first by carrying the Kingdom and presence of God into every environment he enters. Any time I have the opportunity to talk with or meet with Philip, I walk away feeling challenged. Challenged to be more, challenged to pursue God in deeper levels of intimacy, challenged to love and embrace people in more meaningful ways. I recommend, without hesitation, anyone who has a desire to live a lifestyle of worship and tap into the power of God found in that place to read *Worship Without Limits.*

Aaron Davis
Pastor, Author of *The Tattooed Preacher*

True worship is not defined by a geographic location or a certain people group, but by a genuine heart that is hungry for the presence of God. When we learn to apply both spiritual and practical principles to worship, we can truly have worship without limits and freely enjoy the powerful moving of God's Spirit in our midst. Love this from your book.

Jeremiah J. Johnston, PhD
President of Christian Thinkers Society
Resident Institute and Associate Professor of
Early Christianity at Houston Baptist University
Author of *Unimaginable: What Our World Would be Like Without Christianity*
Host of nationally syndicated radio program, *The Jeremiah Johnston Show*

The first time worship is mentioned in the Bible is when Abraham was offering Isaac on the altar. Obedience is true worship. Our Savior Jesus Christ said that the Father is looking for those who worship in spirit and in truth. In *Worship Without Limits,* Philip takes you on a personal journey of what he has learned about worship in his many years of leading others into the presence of God. I enjoyed learning the history of where the worship ministry was founded—the mission field. I loved the focus on worshipping with the Word, the power of humility, and all the practical tips this book provides for worship teams and communities. This book contains chronicles of miracles that God has done when worship was released in the congregation. By finishing each chapter with prayer, Philip allows the reader to be engaged with the Holy Spirit to apply what the reader has learned. This book will change the way you worship.

Pastor Vlad Savchuk
Hungry Generation
www.hungrygen.com/author/pastorvlad

In his book, *Worship Without Limits,* Philip Renner speaks the heart of every pastor I have ever met who has told me his idea of a godly worship leader. Each one is looking for character above music skills. Philip spends much time describing the worship leader's lifestyle of personal worship, fellowship with God, prayer, commitment to unity, teamwork, and submission to authority. These are only a few of the character attributes Philip teaches that produce the anointing in a worship leader's life. You'll love the book and end it with a big "amen."

Pastor Bob Yandian
Author of *Life & Power*

This new book by Philip Renner is not only theologically sound, it's also overflowing with common sense advice for every worship leader and every hungry believer who wants to enter into the deep presence of God in worship. I'm Philip's father, and I am certainly proud of him. But as a fellow minister who is accountable for my words and for what I recommend, I confidently tell you that this is a book worth reading. Every pastor should require his or her worship leader to read it; every worship leader should require everyone in the worship ministry to read it; and all who want to enter the deep places of God should get this book and take its contents deep into their hearts.

Rick Renner
Rick Renner Ministries

WORSHIP WITHOUT LIMITS

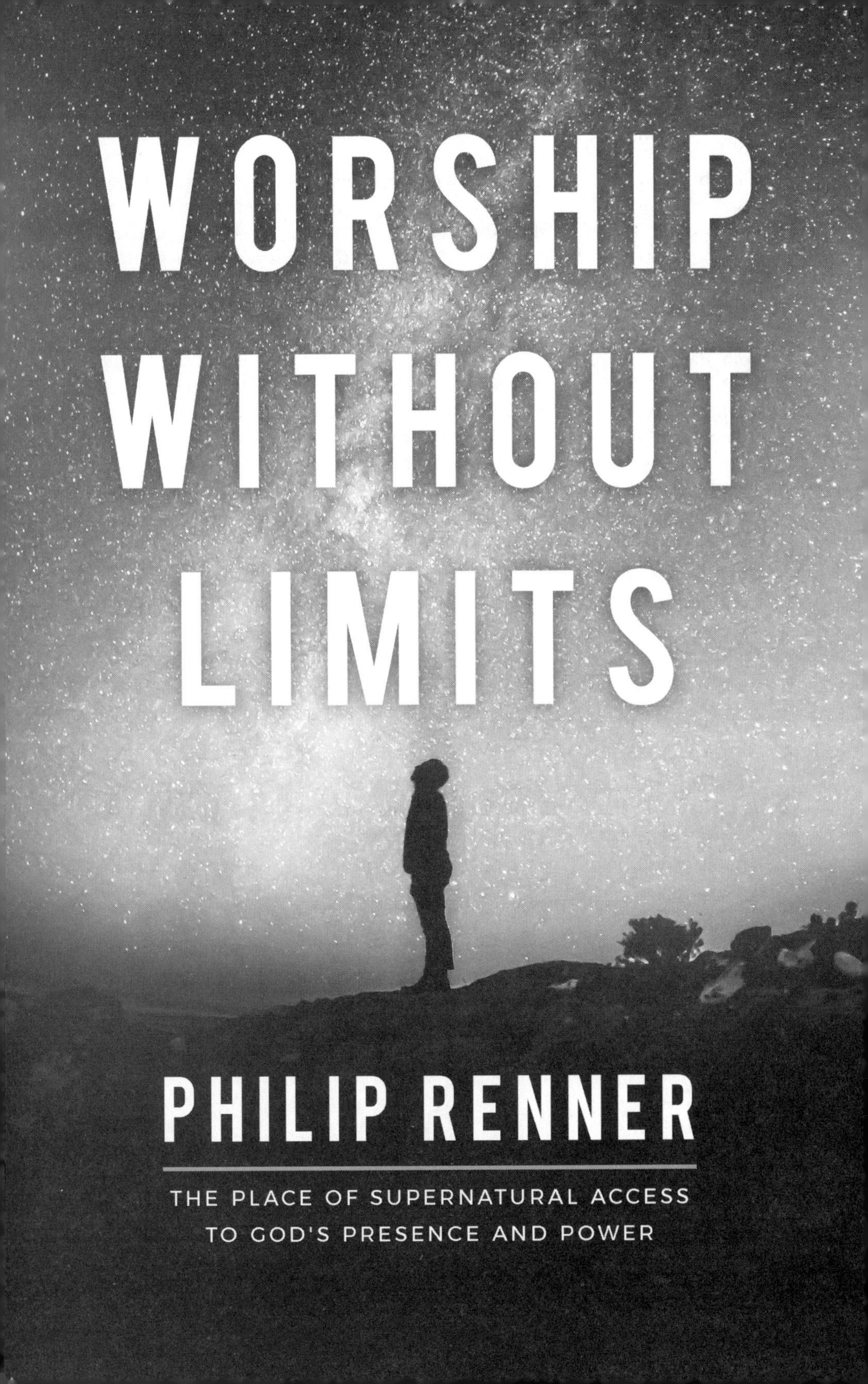

WORSHIP WITHOUT LIMITS

PHILIP RENNER

THE PLACE OF SUPERNATURAL ACCESS TO GOD'S PRESENCE AND POWER

 All emphasis within Scripture quotations is the author's own. Please note that Destiny Image's publishing style capitalizes certain pronouns in Scripture that refer to the Father, Son, and Holy Spirit, and may differ from some publishers' styles. Take note that the name satan and related names are not capitalized. We choose not to acknowledge him, even to the point of violating grammatical rules.

DESTINY IMAGE® PUBLISHERS, INC.
P.O. Box 310, Shippensburg, PA 17257-0310
"Promoting Inspired Lives."

This book and all other Destiny Image and Destiny Image Fiction books are available at Christian bookstores and distributors worldwide.

Cover design byEileen Rockwell
Interior design by Terry Clifton

For more information on foreign distributors, call 717-532-3040.
Reach us on the Internet: www.destinyimage.com.

ISBN 13 TP: 978-0-7684-5082-8
ISBN 13 eBook: 978-0-7684-5083-5
ISBN 13 HC: 978-0-7684-5085-9
ISBN 13 LP: 978-0-7684-5084-2

For Worldwide Distribution, Printed in the U.S.A.
1 2 3 4 5 6 7 8 / 23 22 21 20 19

DEDICATION

My wife and children: I can't say thank you enough! It is because of my wife, Ella, that I can write this book and build the ministry. When I was constantly gone weeks at a time, my wife took care of our wonderful children, Mia and Mika. She has been with me in all kinds of times—good and bad—and she has been a great support through it all. I can honestly say that through my wife's honesty and discernment, God has spoken to me many times. She is a godly, faithful woman, amazing mother, and anointed business lady. Ella, you are an amazing dreamer and you always encourage me to dream bigger. I love you with all of my heart. My wife and children are the reason I race home after every trip. They are my pride and joy.

My Family, Dad—Rick, Mom—Denise, Brothers—Paul and Joel: Dad and Mom you always encouraged me to dream. I can remember from a very young age hearing them say to me "You are a leader!" You instilled the Word of God inside me, which has become the foundation for my life. Thank you all for your support and love.

Renner Worship Band: So many of the principles of this book I understood by experience—experiences I would not trade for anything. Thanks to all of the Renner Worship Band. Together we have laughed, cried, prayed, and fasted on many occasions. You guys are awesome. Specifically, I would like to say thank you to a great musician, composer, and my friend Peter Graznov. We have written so many songs and traveled the world together—love you, brother.

Most importantly I am thankful to Jesus. Thankful for His life given for me. Thankful for my salvation! Thankful for His blood! My one, my all, my everything. I am nothing without You and I owe everything to You—the Lord of lords, King of kings, Ancient of Days, and the great I AM, JESUS.

ACKNOWLEDGMENTS

Pastor Paul and Karen Brady and staff for embracing me into the Millennial family. Thank you for embracing us in our move to the US.

Pastor George and Terri Pearson, Eagle Mountain Church/ KCM Family for your love and support for the whole family. Love you all!

Jeff Fellers for your management and direction for helping me with my ministry and this book, giving me valid input always. For the countless phone calls and time you gave. Thank you for helping me write some vital points.

Kyle Loffelmacher for your belief and friendship and encouragement.

Mica Olinghouse for your amazing insight in editing and direction.

Andrell Corbin for adding crucial insight to Chapter 10 and for being a prayer warrior in my life.

Bob Yandian, a pastor's pastor, thank you for asking me to serve at your Spring Conference and share this message.

Jason Crabb and Tina Morris for sharing my heart and message on TBN.

Phil and Esther Smith and Caleb Eversmith for like hearts for music and ministry.

Joyce Stark and RTP Festival Nashville for hosting my band and music ministry over the years.

Bob Griffin for your support in early US ministry events.

Jason Hollis for your help with the message, connections, and recording the podcast from which this book was formed!

Stefan and Valerie, *The Harvest Show* LeSea TV, for my first US interview.

Jen Rose Yokel for writing an amazing feature in *CCM Magazine.*

Audrey Gray and Artiste Hub for opening doors in the UK.

John and Brittney Jester for your friendship and support.

Pastor Cheryl, George, and family! Bride of Christ Church family is such a blessing.

Wally and June Blume for your support, friendship, and prayers.

Thank you to all my partners who made this book possible—I couldn't have done it without you!

CONTENTS

FOREWORD

Leading worship is more than just leading songs. Worship is about ministering to the heart of God, adoring Him in Spirit and in truth, and inviting people to join you.

What does that look like? Where do you even begin to prepare? Well, you've started at the right place. This book goes into detail of first and foremost the heart of worship; and second, some practical things that will equip you to lead with excellence.

I remember first hearing Philip lead worship in my native tongue on a YouTube video. You see I was always slightly connected to his family in my heart since my family and I moved to the USA from the former Soviet Union. Not knowing much English, we were so happy when we heard of the Renner's ministry at our local church. Philip has been raised in a family full of the truth and the Word of God, and it is reflected in his worship. This book tells a little about his journey.

I believe that just because you can sing does not automatically qualify you to lead worship. In the same way, just because you can speak, does not qualify you to teach the Bible. If you do, you better be ready to carry the weight of responsibility that comes with it. It's not just about how well we sing or play an instrument—it's about how you steward your craft.

Did you know the Levites in the Bible were not allowed to serve in the temple until the age of thirty? All the years before they were training and learning how to steward His presence.

Worship requires excellence and authenticity. How do you cultivate excellence? Practice, discipline, and time. You will not become excellent in your craft overnight. It takes dedication. Why is excellence important? In First Samuel 16:18, it talks about how David played his harp skillfully. What if David went into battle without strengthening his fight? Do you really think that David would've been able to knock the giant down by hitting him in just the right spot had he not been diligent to steward his sling?

When preparing to lead worship, I like to think of it like preparing a battle plan. I also believe that the One who gave us everything, Jesus, deserves our best. If we do not come prepared, then both the congregation as well as the worship leaders are more likely to become distracted and no longer have a vertical focus.

Authenticity. When we come prepared, it allows us to focus on the face of Jesus and truly bring an authentic expression of worship to Him. John 4:24 says to worship the Lord in spirit and in truth. God is Spirit and we are made in His image. We need to become acquainted with the Holy Spirit. Get to know Him as a person. Jesus said that it would be better for Him to ascend into

Heaven, so that we have the opportunity to have the indwelling of the Holy Spirit—to *know* God in such an intimate way.

But how can you lead someone to worship Jesus without knowing Him for yourself. It's more than just reading about Him; it's about spending time communing with Him and worshipping Him in the secret place. I can read every magazine about a celebrity, but that does not mean that I know the person personally. Leading worship has to come from an overflow of your time with Jesus.

Today we have almost got church down to a science. As long as people are singing along and we have enough smoke and good lighting, then we have succeeded. As long as we have people on the platform who look relatable and wear the latest trends, then people can connect. But have we forgotten that worship is about magnifying our King? Worship is about seeking His presence. His presence is what changes things! And when we truly minister to the heart of God, that's what moves His hand toward us. Whether we have a full band or not, whether we have the best sound system or not—if you bless Him, He will draw His people unto Himself.

This book truly points you to the heart of worship and brings you back to the simplicity of what that means. In the Bible it says that Moses would minister to our heavenly Father and come down the mountain with radiating light on his face. May that be the same for us as worship leaders today. May we rise to be the Levites who walk in our authority and enthrone our God upon our praise. May we war with our sound and inspire people to do the same. May we be His reflection.

This book will challenge you and equip you!

Thank you, Philip, for writing a book that equips more leaders to raise a sweet sound to the Father's heart. Thank you for your dedication to God's Word and for setting such a standard in your leadership.

—Anna Byrd
Worship Director
Lifestyle Christianity University
Worship Leader, Gateway Church

CHAPTER 1

THE JOURNEY

When I was six years old, my mother and father moved our family to the former Soviet Union. That's where I grew up—first in Riga, Latvia, and then in Moscow, Russia. That part of the world is where I cut my teeth in the ministry, went to school, made friends, married my wife, and became the father of two beautiful daughters.

Those years in the former USSR also created the context for the opening chapters of my life as a worshipper and eventually a worship leader. What I have learned about worship—the essence and practicalities of it—has been quietly forged in the heart of a young man growing up on the frontlines of the mission field. It has been an indescribable journey and one I'm excited to share with you in this book.

Considering the cultural differences, my story may be quite different from yours, but we all have one thing in common—because of Jesus, we have equal access to God's presence through worship. You may not have had the opportunity to see the world like I did as a young boy, but you have the same access to the Father as I do. The same blood that grants me access grants you access, and the same Spirit who taught me how to worship can teach you! You don't have to grow up in ministry or even in a Christian home to learn how to become a true worshipper. You can celebrate the Father's love and power through His presence in worship, just because you are a child of God.

We all have one thing in common—because of Jesus, we have equal access to God's presence through worship.

One of my earliest memories of experiencing the presence of God through worship happened when I was just five years old. About a year prior to our move overseas, I remember watching my mom sing as she led hundreds of congregations across the United States in worship. Her stunning voice was so loud that I would cover my ears with my hands in the middle of service! Yet in my little boy's heart, I knew people were being touched by God as she projected her operatic voice. Hearing the clapping and testimonies that followed set a fire in my heart to do the same.

As a child, I would often shut the door to my room and pretend to lead people in worship, just like I saw my mother do in the churches we visited. I would pace back and forth in my room, looking at the imaginary crowd and instructing them to lift their hands. How exciting this was for a child with an active imagination! Little did I know then how by pretending to be a worship leader I was actually acting out the dreams in my heart. God's call was evident on my life even from an early age.

Growing up, I continually heard my parents tell me, "Son, you're a leader. You'll do something great for the Kingdom of God." Those words were spoken over me time and time again throughout my childhood and teen years. Finally, those words began to bring a harvest when I turned fifteen.

By that time, my parents were wrapping up their work in Latvia and turning the church over to the next pastor. We had been in Latvia for nine years where my parents, Rick and Denise, had launched the first Christian TV program in the Soviet Union and pioneered a church. Thousands of people were saved and healed as a result of their ministry in that nation. I remember seeing the stacks of letters that continually poured into the office from all over the Russian-speaking community. We received so much mail that I could literally jump into the piles of letters and swim through them as if they were kiddy pools! Rick Renner Ministries was making an amazing impact on that former atheistic corner of the world.

Because I was still young during our time in Latvia, I wasn't able to help in the ministry as much as my older brother Paul. I remember watching him serve in every capacity in the church. He carried sound equipment, worked the sound equipment, and played drums. Paul was so busy helping my parents, and I often wondered when it would be my turn to serve in a more grown-up way.

MY TIME HAD COME

When we moved to Moscow to launch Moscow Good News Church, I had my opportunity. For several years prior, my parents had been growing the church in Latvia. When they turned the leadership over to the associate pastor, we moved to Russia to start the church pioneering process all over again. Since Moscow Good News Church was in its infant stages, it needed a lot of volunteers. And at age fifteen, I was more than willing to step in and help. This was my chance! My time to begin doing what I was called to do had come. In my excitement, I was willing to do anything to serve.

Going to the office and picking up sound equipment at 5 a.m. was so much fun. Looking back at it now, I wouldn't trade those early days of serving in the ministry for anything. Setting up and tearing down every Sunday was part of serving the Lord—and I enjoyed it. I also started carrying the sound equipment, which I considered a great honor. As I was faithful in the little God had given me, more opportunities began coming my way.

Soon, I began to play the trumpet in worship and sing from time to time. In fact, by the time I started singing, I was still playing the trumpet and carrying sound equipment! I was faithful with the little I had, and God continued to add to my plate.

Eventually, I became the youth praise and worship leader. Leading the youth in this capacity became my passion. And just as when I was younger, I began to imagine myself leading thousands of youth in worship all around the world.

At times, I became impatient waiting to see the manifestation of my dreams. I had a huge vision in my heart, but it seemed it was taking a long time to get there! One day God spoke three words to my spirit that changed my life forever—later, better, and different. Those words strengthened me and allowed me to focus on the call. I knew God's best was yet to come!

During that time of leading worship for the youth in my dad's church, God touched my heart in a very special way. I began to love the youth even more, and they eventually started calling me "pastor." Although I loved these young people and felt called to them, I did not think that meant I would become a youth pastor. In fact, I said I would never be the youth pastor! But God had a sense of humor. By the time I was twenty-one, I became the youth pastor of Moscow Good News Church.

The season of youth pastoring was a wonderful time in my life. God taught me many principles that I still implement in ministry today. I learned about the power of fasting and prayer, which have become critical pillars in both my personal and public life. I also learned the importance of discipleship. My heart began to burn for the youth to know God. I wanted to create a culture in our youth group that would facilitate worship and creativity. I encouraged our young people to begin writing their own worship music. As a result, our youth began tapping into the presence of God in a fresh new way.

GOD OPENS UNEXPECTED DOORS IN RUSSIA

It was during this time of youth pastoring when God opened the door for me to evangelize and write music for artists who were influential on Russian music television. This was quite an unexpected twist in my life, but I prayed for God to use me to speak to those in the music world. God answered my prayer, but in a completely different way than I had imagined. I used to think the Lord would use me as a youth speaker or playing music with my band, but God set the stage differently.

I soon became the writer and vocal producer for some well-known Russian artists. Instead of writing about the worldly things they were used to, I wrote about God's standard of morality. In place of sex, I wrote about faithfulness. Instead of hopelessness, I wrote about hope. And guess what? The people I worked with loved it! They didn't know a Christian could be professional, arrive to work on time, work hard, and be a good friend. My witness—through my words and my character—shined brightly for Jesus. And through this avenue, I had many opportunities to talk to professionals in the Russian music industry about the Lord.

When musicians, writers, and producers would start smoking weed in the green room, I would just get out my Bible and start reading. They would ask me what I was doing, and I would reply, "Your source of inspiration, hope, and fun is from drugs—my Source is the Word of God!" Amazingly, these professionals in the world respected me for my boldness and sincerity. They used less profanity around me and didn't tell perverted jokes when I was there. God allowed me to be an influence for righteousness in their lives.

While I was youth pastoring and writing for Russian musicians, I began to write original songs from my personal time with the Lord. After God dropped a message into my spirit, I would first preach it, and then I would sing it. This eventually became the usual pattern of ministry during those early years. I studied hard for the message I was to preach and then just sang what was on my heart.

After a while, I began noticing that people were most affected by the music I was singing. They were ministered to by the preaching as well, but their greatest response was always to the worship. Eventually, this started to ring a bell as I realized my strongest area of anointing was in worship. So, I began to focus more and more on sharpening that particular ministry tool.

My team, Renner Worship, launched our music ministry in a way only God could orchestrate. We finished our worship album with all original songs in Russian and gave it away on social media as a gift to the Russian people. Over the New Year's holiday that year, our songs went viral online. I went to bed one night after posting just eleven worship songs and woke up the next morning to find our songs had been shared thousands of times to churches and groups of all sizes across Russia and Russian-speaking countries. Pretty soon, I began receiving invitations from all over Russia to minister in the Word and worship. My itinerate schedule became so busy that it was hard to continue being a youth pastor. I resigned from my position at the church and passed the youth ministry on to my associate youth pastor.

Before I knew what was happening, we were traveling nine months out of the year to the majority of the former Soviet Union—making regular trips to Latvia, Estonia, Lithuania, Russia, the Ukraine, Belarus, Kazakhstan, Kyrgyzstan, and Armenia. For two years, we saw God do wonderful things. While on the road, our three-hour worship set was followed by demonstrations of the gifts of the Spirit. Many people were being born again, healed, and changed in the presence of God. We saw thousands of people jumping up and down praising God one moment and then laying on their faces before the Lord an hour later. Those nights with the band leading worship across Russian-speaking countries were powerful experiences I'll never forget.

When we traveled, various praise and worship teams from the churches we visited asked us to teach them how to lead worship and write their own songs. So, in addition to leading worship on the stage, we began to lead worship workshops for the churches. Before long, these church teams were writing their own original music! While we started out as one of the only worship movements in Russia, God began raising up other teams and songs wherever our ministry went. What began as a young worship leader traveling Russia with his band turned out to be a catalyst for multiple worship movements all over the former Soviet Union.

GOD STIRS MY HEART FOR THE UNITED STATES

As you can imagine, I was excited and content with all the doors God was opening for me and my ministry in the Russian-speaking community. The ministry there was growing very quickly when suddenly opportunities began to arise to go to the US. My team and I were excited about these new invitations, so we decided to embark on this new adventure.

I do not believe that America could sow missionaries for 200 years all around the world and not reap a bountiful harvest.

When I first went to the States, a burden for revival and supernatural worship began to arise inside me. At the time, it didn't make any sense. Why would I want to leave the wonderful work God was doing in Russia to start all over again in the USA? But as time passed on, that burden for America wouldn't leave; it continued to grow stronger and stronger inside me. Finally, in obedience to the call of God, my wife, children, and I moved to the US. Just as in 1992, America had sown the seed of my parents into the harvest fields of Russia, so now God was using Russia to sow the seeds of my family into the harvest fields of America.

As I travel the US, singing, teaching, leading worship, and training others, I long to see God's people rise up in this nation. I want to see the gifts of the Holy Spirit freely operate in church services. I believe there will be a great outpouring through worship right here in the USA. I do not believe that America could sow missionaries for 200 years all around the world and not reap a bountiful harvest. I believe the greatest move of God is right in front of us. As Christians, we need to be prepared for the work God wants to do; as worship leaders, we need to be able to cooperate fully with the Holy Spirit as He ushers in His greatest work in these last days.

In order to strengthen you as a worshipper and worship leader, I have written this book as a tool to help you prepare for the work God is calling us to in the days ahead. Through my journey as a worship leader, youth pastor, musician, speaker, and writer, I've learned some valuable lessons in Russia that can aptly apply in the United States—and throughout the world. True worship is not defined by a geographic location or a certain people group, but by a genuine heart that is hungry for the presence of God. When we learn to apply both spiritual and practical principles to worship, we can truly have worship without limits and freely enjoy the powerful moving of God's Spirit in our midst.

True worship is not defined by geographic location or a certain people group, but by a genuine heart.

God is continually moving strong worldwide, and I believe He is about to move in an amazing way here in the United States. The future for His Church in America and elsewhere is bright indeed! God is pushing us forward, and I am honored to be part of that push through teaching, preaching, missions, and evangelism wherever I go. When I am not traveling, speaking, and leading worship events on behalf of Philip Renner Ministries, I am honored to serve as worship pastor at Millennial Church in Tulsa, Oklahoma, under Pastor Paul Brady. Here in this house we are praying in revival and pressing into the spirit to see a great outpouring of God's Spirit. God is always with me, as He is with you! Together, we can lead a generation of worshippers into the glorious presence of the Lord.

CHAPTER 2

WORSHIP IS POWERFUL

In pursuing worship without limits, it's important to understand that worship itself is powerful. No matter if it takes place in the privacy of our own homes or on the public stage surrounded by bright lights, if worship comes from a pure heart that is genuinely seeking and magnifying God, it is dynamic, powerful, and transformational. Leaders and laypeople alike can be changed in an instant when they access the presence of God through genuine worship.

Years ago, I asked myself the question, *What makes worship so powerful?* Is it the arrangement and sound? The rhythm? The lights, smoke, production, and stage presence? As I studied and sought the Lord regarding the true impact of worship, I realized that all the natural things are absolutely secondary. While the lights and music make it fun and appealing, these are not the things that truly matter, nor are they what we should prioritize in our worship. What makes worship so powerful and life changing is our own personal relationship with God.

SEEK HIM FIRST

The Bible is very clear that we are to seek God and His Kingdom first. When we are diligent to seek God's ways first, other natural things in life are added to us. Notice Scripture says nothing about seeking the lights or presentation. It doesn't mention anything about orchestrating perfect chords, smoke, or production. It doesn't say anything about those things! It simply says seek God first: *"Seek first the kingdom of God and His righteousness, and all these things shall be added to you"* (Matthew 6:33).

True worship starts when we seek God first and foremost above everything else in life. We have to be worshippers at home first before we're worshippers on stage. What we've developed at home in our private life is what will show up on the public platform.

When we read the Bible, it will read us.

Worship starts for me when I first wake up in the morning. As soon as I open my eyes, the first thing I see is my Bible. It's the first thing I touch and the first thing I read every day. This Book is so powerful, so full of life! It goes into the depths of my heart, changing my thoughts and dreams. Even my family knows not to talk to me if I'm reading my Bible, because studying God's Word is the first priority in my life.

As my dad, Rick Renner often says, "When we read the Bible, it will read us." The Bible will point out things in our lives that need to be changed and conformed to the image of Christ. The

Bible will purify our thoughts and change our dreams, bringing us into alignment with God's purposes. By meditating on the Word, we will receive fresh revelation of who God is and what His plans are for our lives.

It is in that place of study—that holy time of communion with the Father—that the Holy Spirit begins to speak to us and deposit songs from Heaven into our hearts. These are the songs that come up out of our spirit that carry power and anointing. These songs are the ones that flow out from us in worship, the songs that minister to others when we're leading on the stage. True worship—worship that accesses the presence of God and brings others into that glorious place—begins in our own fellowship time with God. The quality and depth of our relationship with the Lord is created moment by moment in that secret place when no one else is looking.

Great music can bring fans, but the anointing brings miracles!

As musicians, we're concerned with chords, presentation, and stage presence, but all the practicalities of music are secondary to the supernatural aspect of fellowshipping with God. If we don't have a relationship with Jesus every day, our music will be a powerless and empty sound that no one needs.

We don't have to put on a show for people. Worship isn't about pleasing people or building a fan base. And the only way we're going to please God is in that secret place where no one else is watching. *Great music can bring fans, but the anointing brings miracles!*

Sometimes, believers feel they have to brag on what they're doing for God. They may say, "Oh, I'm fasting. Oh, I'm praying.

Look how horrible I look. I'm so spiritual! Look at all I'm doing to sacrifice for God." In reality, all our bragging does is reveal a place of spiritual pride.

We can fast and pray and not have to tell a single soul what we're doing. Why? Because our goal is not to show others how great we are—but rather to honor God. He's the One who's watching, and He's the One who rewards.

Matthew 6:5-6 (NIV) says:

> *And when you pray, do not be like the hypocrites, for they love to pray standing in the synagogues and on the street corners to be seen by others. Truly I tell you, they have received their reward in full. But when you pray, go into your room, close the door and pray to your Father, who is unseen. Then your Father, who sees what is done in secret, will reward you.*

What's done in secret blesses God's heart, not the actions that are done publicly.

The most important thing we do in life is what we do in secret in our walk with God. It is our private relationship with the Lord that matters most!

SATURATED LIKE A SPONGE

When we seek God in the morning, we should become saturated like a sponge with Him. We are to become so saturated with the presence of God during our private times that when we're in public, His presence just flows out from us. If we truly want to bring others into the presence of God, we must learn how to flow with His Spirit first in our daily lives, away from public view.

Have you ever had God wake you up and say, "I want to talk to you"? What did you do? Did you roll over and go back to sleep, because you wanted sleep more than you wanted God? What about during those times in the day when the Lord whispers to your heart, "Come talk to Me"? Do you follow His voice and spend time with Him, or do you ignore His leading to spend time with your friends and hobbies?

Learning to respond to God's invitation of fellowship is critical to becoming a true worshipper. We're in big trouble if we don't have time to talk with God! He's the Creator of the universe; He holds everything in His hands. If anyone is going to understand our life and the way it's supposed to flow and function, it's God.

Learning to respond to God's invitation of fellowship is critical to becoming a true worshipper.

So, when God says, "Come talk to Me," we had better respond immediately! Our willingness to fellowship with God during those private hours prepares us for leading others on stage. The more we allow ourselves to become saturated in God's presence, the more we have to give out to others. What we put in us is what will be squeezed out from us!

Not only will time with the Word make a difference in our personal life, it will also make a tremendous impact in how we lead worship. The Word we've been putting in ourselves during those private times with God may come out through singing a solo or playing the drums. People may even say, "Wow! That song was so different!" And we'll know exactly why our music was different from before. We've been saturating ourselves in the Word! God's power came through us because it has been building up in us all week long.

TRUE WORSHIP IS A LIFESTYLE

True worship is not just something we do on stage; it's a lifestyle. It's a lifestyle when we get up, a lifestyle when we go to bed, a lifestyle in the movies and music we choose. It's a lifestyle in the way we speak to our parents, our kids, our coworkers, and our employers. Worship is a lifestyle that reflects God's glory to those around us in every situation every day.

True worship is not just something we do on stage.

In order for worship to be pure and genuine, it must flow from the Source of living water. Worship that's been contaminated by other influences—other than God's Spirit—is polluted and powerless. Polluted water doesn't have the ability to change people, bring healing, or produce peace. Only worship that flows from living water can transform people and bring them into a place of connection with God.

Notice what John 4:14 (NIV) says: *"whoever drinks the water I give them will never thirst. Indeed, the water I give them will become in them a spring of water welling up to eternal life."* Water flowing from God's Spirit is what brings life!

The music of the world will never fill the void in people's lives. No matter how great the chords or instrumentation are, people will always leave thirsty. It is only God's Spirit who can satisfy the human heart.

As much as presentation is important, it's not the answer. Great rhythm, lyrics, stage presence, lights—all of these things are great, but they are not the primary ingredients to worship. What brings the power and changes people's lives is our personal relationship with Jesus.

If we've gone through our whole week, neglecting our time with the Lord, we'll have nothing to give during our time of leading worship on Sunday. If we're an empty sponge, then guess what? We have nothing to pour out when we're squeezed! Because what we put in our hearts is what comes out, we must actively put the Word in us on a daily basis. That's what will satisfy others!

No matter how great the chords or instrumentation are, people will always leave thirsty. It is only God's Spirit who can satisfy the human heart.

Now here's the thing—once a sponge is squeezed, it has to fill back up again. When we fill up our hearts with God's Word and His presence Monday, Tuesday, Wednesday, and throughout the week, we have something big inside us to give out on Sunday. But once we've led others in worship during the service, we've emptied ourselves of everything we've been putting in all week. So, we have to fill ourselves back up again! On and on this goes... saturate and squeeze, saturate and squeeze. We must continually saturate ourselves so that we can continually give out living water to others.

I encourage you—especially if you are a musician—to restructure your paradigm. Tradition may have taught you to put the music and performance first, even in times of leading worship, but worship without the presence of God is powerless. Instead of seeking the natural things first, begin putting God first. Wake up every morning with a desire to seek after God and His Word. Spend time in His presence. Be like a sponge and saturate yourself in God every day.

Then, when the time comes for you to lead worship on the platform, you'll have something to give to people. When you've sought the Kingdom of God first, you'll be able to truly lead people into the presence of God. No longer will worship be a natural outlet for your gifts and talents; it will become a supernatural instrument of power because you've been seeking God in the secret place. If you put your relationship with God first—above the music, above the talents, above the lights—God will use you to bring people into a powerful place of intimacy with Him.

PRAYER

Father God, I'm tired of worship just being a concert without power. I want Your power to be manifested when we worship You. I don't want to please people; I want to please You. When I play or sing, I want You to be glorified.

Lord, I understand the natural things are secondary to the spiritual. Because Your Word says to seek You first, I'm going to begin seeking You above all else in life. Every day as I spend time with You and Your Word, I ask You to saturate me with Your glory, Your power, and Your anointing. I understand that nothing compares to my relationship with You. Without personal time with You, everything else is empty, and I have nothing to give to others.

God, I repent for not seeking You first. I commit today to put You first in my life, in my relationships, and in my music. Fill my talent with Your glory and power. As I seek You first, You will add everything else I need.

I thank You for teaching me to flow with Your Spirit. The next time I go on stage, I will be filled with Your power! I will fulfill the assignment You have given me because I have made You first in my life.

In Jesus' name, amen.

CHAPTER 3

THE FOUNDATION OF WORSHIP

To build a strong worship ministry in any church, it's important to lay a solid foundation first. We must understand what true worship is, where it flows from, and what it produces. Without knowing the basic principles that govern worship, our worship will never extend any higher or deeper than it does now. If we are pursuing worship without limits, then we must begin at the foundation—at the very place from where worship begins.

In many churches, the standard service structure starts off with a count-down video, a time of greeting, or a great music set. While all of these things are good, none of them release God's power or set the stage for His presence to flow in our midst. Not even a great music intro establishes the proper foundation for a powerful time in worship.

So where should worship begin? John 1:1 says this: *"In the beginning was the Word, and the Word was with God, and the Word was God."* Powerful worship is established by the Word of God.

REACHING A BIBLICALLY ILLITERATE GENERATION

Because we live in a post-modern world that is biblically illiterate, the first step in laying the groundwork for transformational worship is pointing people to the foundation of God's Word for their own spiritual growth and development. When people have no understanding of even the basic principles of the Bible, leaders are saddled with an enormous responsibility to teach and preach the simple truths of God's Word. True worship is limited when the congregation is missing its foundation in the Word, because the Bible says true worshippers must worship God *"in the Spirit and in truth"* (John 4:24 NIV). Truth is the Word of God.

True worship is limited when the congregation is missing its foundation in the Word.

When I lived in Russia, people came to our church from all kinds of different backgrounds and cultures. Not surprisingly, most of our congregation over the age of forty grew up under the communist regime of the Soviet Union. Because that system was anti-God and anti-Bible, people knew very little of God's Word. As a result, our family had to firmly establish them in the truth of the Bible. It was critical to the success of our church to show the Russian people how they could trust God's authority as revealed in His written Word. As part of their spiritual formation, they had to know how to read the Bible for themselves and how to apply it to their everyday lives.

Thankfully, the Lord has graced my father with a tremendous teaching gift, which has equipped him well for his ministry assignment in Russia. By using his extensive knowledge of the

Greek language, he takes apart every Scripture to illuminate its meaning so people can understand it and then repent in order to walk accurately in the resurrection power of Christ.

While my dad's ministry is specialized to Russian Christians, his teaching is also relevant to the American and worldwide Church as well. You can learn more about his ministry or purchase his books and teaching materials by visiting his website at renner.org. I highly recommend his materials for youth and youth pastors. Young people need more than just funny stories—they need strong teaching that will ground them in their faith. This kind of ministry is what will feed their spirits instead of entertaining their flesh.

When I moved back to the United States, I found an interesting parallel between the young generation in the US and the older communist generation in Russia. Interestingly enough, the current spiritual crisis facing today's young people in the United States is similar to that of the older Soviet generation. Sure, young people in the US may not have grown up under a communist system, but they have been inundated with a social, media, and political culture that is anti-God and anti-Bible. Sadly, most millennials don't even know some of the most basic stories in the Bible!

The current spiritual crisis facing today's young people in the United States is similar to that of the older Soviet generation.

According to a report in *Christianity Today,* Generation Y and Z are less likely to read or trust the Bible than previous generations. Other statistics have revealed that millennials are the most unchurched, least faith-identified, and least exposed to the Gospel of any generation in our nation's history. More than half of them are described as "Bible-neutral" or "Bible-skeptical." What they know about Christians and Christianity in general is formed from the negative slant they read on social media or hear in the news.

We are at a tipping point in reaching Millennials, and only truth from God's Word can pull this generation from darkness into light.

The abysmal lack of God's truth present in American millennials should compel every leader, pastor, and believer to uplift the standard of the Bible in our churches and worship services. This is why we have an urgent calling to speak the Word. Only God's truth is the final authority that has the power to set people free from the bondage of sin. It is the only sure foundation! By building our worship on the Word of God, we have an opportunity to teach young people what the Bible says and to show them how to understand God's truth.

I have a passion to reach this generation because they are the future of the Church. Relevance has been the buzz word in recent years at various conferences, festivals, and events, but what impact has that had? We are at a tipping point in reaching Millennials, and only truth from God's Word can pull this generation from darkness into light.

One thing I can tell you about millennials is they crave authentic community and are open to experiencing God in a profound and supernatural way. I believe there is a huge vacuum of authentic, Spirit-filled ministry reaching out to this generation. More than ever, those of us who know God's truth and His Spirit must rise up in this hour to minister to our own age group.

I want to challenge you to answer this call to take God into your generation. Will you do it? Will you put your own agenda aside and reach out to young people both inside and outside of your church?

Perhaps you are a member of a band that plays at events attended by a non-Christian crowd. You may be the only Jesus someone sees or hears in that situation. Be bold to share your testimony and what Jesus has done for you! If you're willing to stand up for Jesus, God will open doors for you to boldly speak for Him. You may be surprised one day when someone comes up to you after a show and says, "Your music was cool, but I really related to what you said about forgiving others and myself. Are you a Christian? My mom has been praying for me since I left home, and what you said really spoke to me." Opportunities to minister to your generation are all around if you're willing to be used by the Lord.

Having a Bible foundation is so important in our lives because people are waiting to hear the truth that sets them free. We don't have a lack of technology or an absence of Christian music in our churches today, but we *do* have a lack of a biblical worldview. So much of what is presented in our churches has been reduced to entertainment with no scriptural accountability and a powerless, formulated message. We need the pure Word of the Bible preached in power and demonstrated by the fire of the Holy Spirit!

BEGIN WORSHIP WITH THE WORD

Therefore, as a music leader, potential worship leader, or someone seeking your place in God's will, one of the most critical things you can do to set the tone for a time of transformational worship is to begin by quoting the Word of God. As discussed in the previous chapter, it is your personal relationship with God's Word that makes worship powerful. In the same manner, public worship also flows from a relationship with God's Word. By honoring God's Word at the very beginning of a worship service, you create an environment based on truth, established on God's promises, and one that releases faith into the atmosphere.

Before you begin leading people into worship, remember to start off with Scripture.

So, before you begin leading people into worship, remember to start off with Scripture. I like to call this the *First Rule of Leading Worship: Start with Scripture.* This can be a Scripture you've been meditating on during the week, a Scripture the pastor has been ministering on in recent messages, or a Scripture that relates to the songs you've chosen for the worship set. It may even be a Scripture the Holy Spirit drops in your heart right before service! And because you've been diligent to saturate yourself with the Word all week, you'll always have a verse to share as you lead the congregation, small group, or Bible study into worship. When you do this, it creates unity among the people—and where unity exists, miracles happen and God touches hearts.

When you come to the service prepared with a Scripture to give at the onset of worship, you are establishing a higher perspective. People have been through all kinds of stuff during the week; but the moment you begin to speak forth the Word of God, they get their minds off their problems and focus on God. This is a moment for creating connection and unity. No matter what you, the band, or the congregation have experienced prior to this point, this is the time you all lay those distractions aside and come into faith and unity.

Of course, you can greet the people and ask them to shake hands with those around them. But people can meet and greet anytime and anywhere. What the congregation needs from you at this moment in the service is encouragement. They need to be reminded of who God is and what His Word says. If you can make this adjustment in your leadership and open up worship with the Word, people will follow you into worship much easier because their focus has been properly redirected to the Word.

This practice of building worship on the foundation of the Word can be carried through the entire worship set from start to finish. For example, take advantage of a transition time from one song to another to speak a word to the people. Don't let it be just a musical piece—let it be a time of encouragement and edification for the Body of Christ. A piano solo is beautiful, but an accompanying word or Scripture with the piano solo is much more powerful!

THE WORD IN SPONTANEOUS SONG

Another way to prioritize the Word in worship is to make room for the Holy Spirit to bring a specific Scripture in spontaneous song. The Bible instructs us about spontaneous singing in Ephesians 5:19 (Amplified Bible, Classic Edition): *"Speak out to one another in psalms and hymns and spiritual songs, offering praise with voices [and instruments] and making melody with all your heart to the Lord."* Colossians 3:16 (Amplified Bible) clarifies this point even more:

> *Let the [spoken] word of Christ have its home within you [dwelling in your heart and mind—permeating every aspect of your being] as you teach [spiritual things] and admonish and train one another with all wisdom, singing psalms and hymns and spiritual songs with thankfulness in your hearts to God.*

Often spontaneous singing may break out when the Spirit of God is moving in a specific way or is endeavoring to bring revelation along a certain truth. Whenever this happens, I suggest putting your own agenda aside, stepping out in faith, and obeying the Holy Spirit. You may never know what blessings are on the other side of your obedience!

Not too long ago, I had an experience with spontaneous singing that happened in a service in my home church in Tulsa. A guest speaker was preaching about God's resurrection power, and the Holy Spirit began to move among the people. The minister then began praying for a woman in a wheelchair. At first, she seemed to gain some healing, but she did not have the strength to walk by herself. In anticipation for her complete healing, the speaker told her to sit in a chair on the front row and to wait for a time in the service when she would spontaneously walk and be completely healed.

As the minister continued preaching, this passage from Matthew 18:18 began rolling around in my heart: "*Whatsoever ye shall bind on earth shall be bound in heaven: and whatsoever ye shall loose on earth shall be loosed in heaven.*" That Scripture became so strong in my spirit that I began to quietly sing it, increasing my volume as I sang it over and over. I thought to myself, *This is disrupting the service!* Finally, I got loud enough that my pastor heard it. He quickly gave me an extra mic, and I began to sing out a spontaneous song from Matthew 18:18 (KJV).

When we began singing the Word, the impossible became possible.

The singing then turned into a cry and a declaration. As I continued with the spontaneous song, I watched the woman who was in the wheelchair on the front row get up and start running across the auditorium. It was a complete miracle!

When we began singing the Word, the impossible became possible. That broken lady received her healing that day because the Word of God was sung over her. As a result of our obedience to step out in faith and sing a spontaneous song from the Word, we witnessed God bring healing, encouragement, and restoration.

KEY TO GOD'S POWER

In developing your leadership as a worship minister, or even a more liberated worshipper, remember that the foundation for true worship is not music, lights, media, or presentation. Those things are great enhancements, but they are not the structural foundation for transformational worship. The only solid foundation to grow and build on is God's Word. As you prioritize the Word in your worship—from the opening, through the musical transitions, and all the way to the end—you'll create an unshakeable atmosphere in which the Holy Spirit can move in a dynamic way.

Using Scripture in between songs and speaking out the Word as you lead is actually helping the pastor reach people. You are preparing the harvest so that the pastor can come and gather it. In using the Word, you are working as team with your pastor, which is something all pastors will very much appreciate. As a worshipper, it is your calling to praise and give God all the glory He deserves. Likewise, as a worship leader, it is your calling to help your pastor build the church through worship.

The Word unifies the congregation, edifies the people, builds up faith, and releases power.

Remember, the Word unifies the congregation, edifies the people, builds up faith, and releases power. It is the only foundation for *worship without limits!*

PRAYER

Father God, I commit to change my thinking and my mindset about worship. I will not build my life or my worship on natural things, but on Your Word alone. Your Word is the only strong, unshakeable foundation for worship.

From now on, I will come to service prepared in the Word. I thank You for giving me Scriptures to share with the people during every worship service. As I saturate myself in Your Word and yield to Your Spirit, Your words will flow out of my heart, through my mouth, and edify everyone present.

Lord, help me to be a great worshipper or worship leader who brings people into Your presence. As I put God's Word first during worship, I know the focus won't be on me or on the stage, but on You, because You are the One we worship. Jesus, I honor and love You and Your Word!

I also lift up my generation to You, Lord. Help me to share the truth of God's Word to people my own age so they can know You like I do. Raise up leaders to minister to students and young adults in a way that they can receive and understand. I thank You for a mighty harvest among my peers. We will rise up in God's glory and power in this hour, because we've been called into the Kingdom for such a time as this.

In Jesus' name, amen.

CHAPTER 4

CHANGING THE ATMOSPHERE THROUGH WORSHIP

Have you ever been in a church service that went right into teaching the Word without first setting aside time for worship? Probably not. In fact, most church services always start off with worship. Why? Because worship lays the foundation for the service and sets the tone for the delivery of the Word.

As discussed in the last chapter, worship that is infused with Scripture brings people into unity as they lay aside their problems and focus on God. No matter what people are going through—sickness in their bodies, worry in their minds, or even conflict in their personal relationships—worship gives them an opportunity to turn their eyes away from the issues and onto the solution. When grounded in the Word, worship has such powerful potential to lift people out of their mess and into a place of faith and unity.

Now, let's take a look at what happens to the atmosphere around people when they begin to come together in worship. At first, when everyone walks through the church door, they are carrying all kinds of secret baggage—marriage problems, identity issues, worries, discouragement, pride, selfishness, etc. Most people aren't focused on God—they're trying to figure out life, wondering how they're going to pay their bills, or even nursing a broken heart. All of these worries and cares of life create a corporate atmosphere filled with discouragement, fear, or anxiety.

Most people aren't focused on God—they're trying to figure out life, wondering how they're going to pay their bills, or even nursing a broken heart.

However, when people begin to worship and change their focus, something happens...the atmosphere begins to change and shift. As people are lifted out of their problems in their minds, their moods lighten. The frowns on their faces turn into smiles. The sadness they first carried into the sanctuary melts away. The anger toward their spouse dissipates. As the congregation magnifies Jesus through worship, the heavy atmosphere that once permeated the building is now replaced with joy, unity, and peace.

In fact, the Hebrew word for "praise" is *tehillah,* which means "change in the atmosphere." When people come together in praise and worship, raising their hands, shouting praises to God, they are changing the atmosphere. Something spiritual happens. It's not just some cool music evoking emotions—it's the act of worship and the presence of God that changes lives.

Worship has a powerful potential to change the atmosphere because it changes people's focus, exalts Jesus, and ushers in the presence of God. Even just a few moments in the presence of God through worship can reset a discouraging atmosphere!

Thanks to the power of the Holy Spirit, you and your worship team also have the potential to change the atmosphere in the city where you live. You can influence the political or economic situation in a country by breaking through in worship. Worship has the power to literally change, adjust, and transform any atmosphere! That is what *tehillah* in the Hebrew is all about!

CHANGING THE ATMOSPHERE—DON'T BELIEVE THE WEATHER REPORT

I've personally witnessed how worship can change the spiritual and natural atmosphere around us—including the weather. I was invited to lead an outdoor event by a Baptist church an hour from Nashville, Tennessee. This was an outreach event that the church's young adults' class organizes. Rehearsal the day before was with local volunteer musicians I had never worked with before. The rehearsal went smoothly and we were filled with anticipation until we heard the weather forecast. It was supposed to rain the next day during the event—a devastating report for an outdoor event!

Worship has the power to literally change, adjust, and transform any atmosphere!

The next day, we started setting up the stage and then came the rain. The volunteer musicians, whom I had not worked with before, looked at me and said, "I guess nothing is going to work out." I said, "No, we will play. God wants to change the lives of those who could be impacted."

As we prayed together before worship. I said, "God, as we worship, I ask You to change the atmosphere." These musicians looked at each other and honestly kinda laughed. I just confidently said to these musicians, "Jesus spoke to the wind, so why can't we?" Mark 4:39 (Contemporary English Version) says, *"Jesus got up and ordered the wind and the waves to be quiet. The wind stopped, and everything was calm."*

As we started playing, God answered our prayer, and the rain stopped. People started coming from the surrounding neighborhood. One teenager said he walked twelve blocks looking for the sound that he heard and finally he found it. God touched lives that day!

There are people who have a sound, and that sound will attract others. It is the sound of the army of God arising and people run to it from everywhere. Being part of worship is being part of that sound.

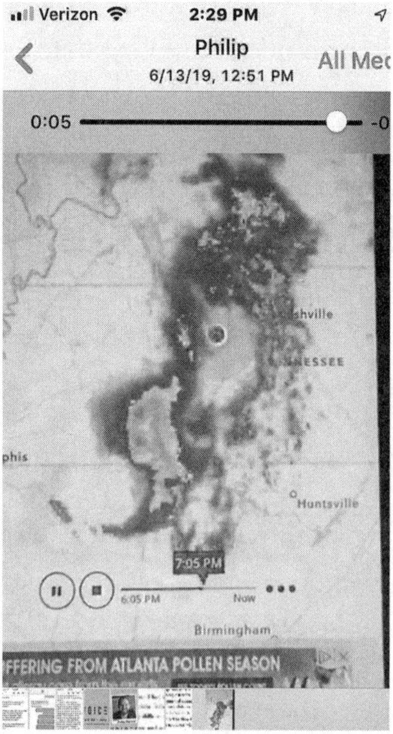

It was a great event that day. I thanked God for it. When we were celebrating and eating after the event, one of the musicians said, "Philip, did you hear what happened with the rain?" I said, "Yeah, it stopped when we started to worship." He said, "Yes, Philip, but it continued to rain all over, the only place it was *not r*aining was the area where we were worshipping." Then he showed me the satellite image that proved it. Sure enough, rain was everywhere except there was a clear spot over right where we had our event!

Why, did God change the physical atmosphere at the event? Because God wanted to touch people's lives in that neighborhood. That is what worship and ministry is about, changed lives! I believe when we worship not only the physical atmosphere changes but also the economic and political atmosphere changes in neighborhoods, cities, and nations!

All God needs are people to connect with Him in Spirit and in truth. One holy moment of worship where you are singing what Heaven is singing changes everything. Worship brings us to a place of great unity as the Body of Christ. When this happens, things begin to shift and change. Get ready for a great shift in the Body of Christ. We are all coming together regardless of denomination or background and the atmosphere is about to change.

YOU'RE A LEADER!

It's important for you to understand the power released when you worship God in Spirit and in truth. When leading worship, you play an integral role in facilitating this wonderful change in the corporate environment. That's why it's critical you come to church prepared and prayed up—just as much as the pastor—because God has placed a responsibility on you to be a catalyst for change.

I think of a praise and worship leader as someone who is leading the sheep. In fact, I like to call this the *Second Rule of Worship: Leading People into Worship and the Presence of God.*

You're not just a nice singing voice on the stage with a mic and lights; you're to be both an example and leader in the area of worship, character, and holiness.

Everything you do as a worship leader has the potential to bring people deeper into God's presence. For example, when you encourage people to lift their hands, you're helping them bring God a sacrifice of praise. When you're exhorting the people with Scripture, you're providing them with the solution to their problems. When you say, "Turn to your neighbors and tell them what God has done in your life this week," you are giving people an opportunity to testify—or to give voice to their testimony. This in itself releases the power of God into the lives of people (see Revelation 12:11). Each direction and encouragement you give from the platform helps people to make that connection to the Spirit of God during service. You're more than a musician—you're a leader!

You're not just a nice singing voice on the stage with a mic and lights; you're to be both an example and leader in the area of worship, character, and holiness.

As a worship leader, your primary function in the service and in the Body of Christ at large is to lead people into a deeper place of the Spirit. However, this progression doesn't happen just through music—it's done by leading the people. You lead the people, and the people follow you. What an honor and privilege to serve God and the Church in this capacity!

Because the Lord has so carefully placed you in such a powerful catalyst position, you must take your calling very seriously. This is why it's so important for you to maintain a consistently fresh relationship with the Lord every day. God is counting on you to help lead others into His presence! Being a worship leader isn't about status or control—it's about humility, obedience, and service. Through your heart, your talents, and your relationship with God, you have this incredible honor to be a gatekeeper in the house of the Lord.

Now with that in mind, I want to encourage you to look at your time leading worship in a whole new way. You're not just a voice or a musician, you're a leader of worship. People won't worship in the service by themselves; you have to lead the people into worship. They have to be taught correctly and led into it properly.

I have ministered in many places where people do not want to praise; but as soon as they are taught *why* we praise, everything changes. Christians need to be reminded of the significance of lifting our hands, declaring the Word of God, and praising the Lord through worship. For example, I may take twenty seconds teaching the congregation that lifting hands in worship is symbolic of surrendering their lives, passions, and dreams to the Lord. This is a simple but powerful truth that takes little time off the clock to explain. By reiterating the why and how of worship, I've helped bring clarity and understanding to people so they can enter into the presence of God more fully. (See Psalm 144:1.) This verse states that our hands are weapons of war, so when you we lift our hands we are not only changing the spiritual atmosphere, we are waging war in the spirit with our hands.

Exhorting people and leading them as you worship is something you can do with simplicity and brevity. You don't have to take ten minutes out of the song set to teach them—just simply share a power nugget of truth in one minute or less. It's amazing how people will grow in their understanding of worship if you will teach them as you go.

Don't always assume people know what the Bible says about worship, because many times they have no clue.

I encourage you to begin making exhortation and teaching a habit in your leadership. Don't always assume people know what the Bible says about worship, because many times they have no clue. Take the opportunity you have while on stage to teach them the basics of biblical worship. If you do this, you will find that people will enter into worship more freely and readily because they understand the *why* and *how* of worship.

LEADERSHIP IS MORE THAN MUSICIANSHIP

An effective praise and worship leader is not just a good singer or a knowledgeable musician. This person is also a teacher, instructor, and a leader. I've been in many services where the music is awesome, but because the person leading wasn't leading effectively, the worship didn't go where it was supposed to go. It didn't reach the height or the depth that it had the potential to reach. In cases like this, the worship leader is only carrying out a musical duty instead of leading people into worship. The leader is not leading or teaching, but simply singing. There's a big difference!

An effective praise and worship leader is not just a good singer or a knowledgeable musician.

So, whether you're on a platform, in a small group, or wherever, lead people into worship by example. If you know it's time to shout to God, tell the people to shout! Show them how to do it by shouting the victory. Set the example before them. This will take more effort from you, but it will help release faith into the people. When you know it's time to enter into a deeper place of worship, set the example. Instruct the people by saying, "Let's get on our knees and cry out before God." As you instruct them through your words and actions, you are teaching people not only how to worship but also how to flow with the Spirit of God as He moves in various ways.

Of course, leading worship by example will require more effort from you. You may not always feel like personally demonstrating actions of worship; but remember, you are a leader. You are the one who charts the course and sets the tone. By exemplifying worship in a humble way before the people, you are helping to release faith in them. When they see their leaders worship, they will be more inclined to follow suit. If you worship first, people will follow!

Once you learn to lead people effectively into worship, you may be tempted to think more highly of yourself than you should. I know from personal experience how easy it is to get lifted into pride when you see the fruit of your leadership. It's imperative to keep your eyes on Jesus and resist the devil when he begins speaking to your pride.

Many times as I have led worship, I've heard the devil whisper in my ear, "You're doing so good. These people wouldn't be here without you." He's tried to appeal to my success and the fruit of my labor. At first, I was tempted to believe his lies, but then the realization rose up in my spirit—the fruit and success is all because of Jesus! I am just a vessel yielded unto Him!

As worship leaders, we must learn to discern the devil's tactics and resist his efforts. Anytime we are tempted to step over into pride, we have to tell the devil, "Get behind me, satan! This isn't me at all. I'm just a vessel God is using. Without God, I am nothing. Without His love, I am nothing. Without God, without His power, without His glory, and without His leading, all of this would be an empty sound." As long as we keep our eyes on Jesus and make Him the center, the devil can't trap us with pride.

TO LEAD, YOU MUST UNDERSTAND

In order to be an effective worship leader who cooperates with the Spirit of God and helps lead the charge in changing the atmosphere, you must first understand the basics of worship. You can't teach others to worship effectively if you don't learn scriptural principles first. Before you can ever begin to lead people into a place of powerful worship, you need to understand what the Word says about how and why we worship.

Sometimes, people in the Church think that some of our charismatic practices were borrowed from the world. But let me assure you, the Scripture has already settled these issues. Whenever you're in doubt about something, make it a practice to go back to the Word and find out what it says. If you build your worship practices on the Word, you'll stay steady and free from error or excess.

For example, people often have questions about the practice of raising our hands during worship. Some even think we've "stolen" this practice from the world. But if we go back to the Word, we find out that God instructs us to lift up our hands as an act of worship and surrender. Psalm 134:2 (NIV) says, *"Lift up your hands in the sanctuary and praise the Lord."* Psalm 28:2 states, *"Hear the voice of my supplications When I cry to You, when I lift up my hands toward Your holy sanctuary."* Worshipping with hands raised is a biblical practice that started in God's temple, not in the world.

Actually, what we see in rock concerts and things in the world are actually practices that have been stolen from the Church and then perverted and twisted to glorify humans instead of God. But is it any wonder? Lucifer was actually the praise and worship leader in Heaven! He knows music. And when Lucifer was kicked out of Heaven, he took all his music abilities and knowledge and twisted them, filling them with pride, perversion, and self-glorification. (See Ezekiel 28:12-19 and Isaiah 14:12-15.)

So as worship leaders, we have an opportunity to reintroduce worship in its pure form as God intended. Instead of letting music and worship become people-focused or people-driven, we protect its purity and restore its proper place and usage in the house of God.

As worship leaders, we have an opportunity to reintroduce worship in its pure form as God intended.

As you're standing on the platform and taking those moments to teach people how to worship, remember you are showing people what the Word says about worship. When you instruct the congregation to lift up their hands, you're encouraging them to implement the Word in their worship. You're showing them how to surrender their dreams and their fears, their failures and their successes to the Lord. By lifting your hands, you're showing others how to symbolically lift up all their cares and worries to God.

Nothing else matters but Him and His greatness. He is the One to glorify!

And when we begin to worship God in complete surrender, we are also telling the devil who is Lord in our lives. We are exalting God above all. Even when everything is going wrong in our lives, when we're sick or when we're sad, by worshipping Jesus with our voices and our uplifted hands, we are drawing a battle line in the sand. We're saying, "Devil, you can try to hit me one more time, but I'm still standing because the name of Jesus is a strong tower. You can try anything you want, but the victory is mine because God is standing with me. There is an anchor to my faith, and it's Jesus Christ. And He is always lifting me up!"

Isaiah 8:10 (NIV) says, *"Devise your strategy, but it will be thwarted; propose your plan, but it will not stand, for God is with us."* By the power of God and through the blood of Jesus, you can abort whatever evil strategies the devil may try to plot against you. Remember, the devil is a liar and a loser! Jesus Christ is on your side; and with Him, you can overcome every trap of the enemy.

YOU'RE AN AMBASSADOR

Whenever you're on that stage leading others in worship, remember you are an ambassador for Christ (see 2 Corinthians 5:20). You're not standing there representing yourself or your interests, but you are reflecting Jesus and His purposes.

Because you're an ambassador for Christ, you can carry the authority to stand in the place God called you to be. As you're submitted to Christ and the pastoral leadership of that house, you can boldly teach and demonstrate to others how to worship

God correctly. Don't be ashamed to instruct others how to worship. You're nobody without God, but with God you are more than a conqueror! (See Romans 8:31-37.) He has empowered and equipped you to lead effectively in the area of worship.

Remember, you're not just a singer or musician—you're a teacher and a leader. You have been called and anointed to show people how to enter into God's presence fearlessly and humbly. Just like a shepherd, you can lead the people by the hand in a Spirit of truth and purity. People are looking to you to show them how to flow with the Spirit of God in worship. And if you stick with the Word and are submitted to Christ's authority, you can show people the way into the deep, sweet places of the Spirit of God.

You're not just a singer or musician—you're a teacher and a leader.

Worship has an incredible potential to change the atmosphere, but it takes quality leadership to lead people into the presence of God. You have an opportunity, an honor, and a great responsibility to chart the course and elevate the atmosphere through worship. Not only is God with you to help you do your part, He is also counting on you to cooperate with Him in this great adventure. So don't back down from this responsibility; step up to the plate and lead the charge!

PRAYER

Father God, You are the God of all wisdom. You know exactly how we are to worship You. You know when we are to raise our hands or fall down on bended knee. I thank You for the Holy Spirit who teaches me as I teach others how to worship You effectively.

I thank You that You will give me the Scriptures I need to lead the people. I commit to follow You as You lead me. I ask You to show me how to instruct people at each point of the worship service. I will keep my spirit open to Your Spirit, and when He says do this, I will do it.

Lord, I thank You for teaching me how to lead people into Your presence. I know that worship is a powerful catalyst that changes the atmosphere. I want to cooperate with You as we take adventures in worship. I am Your vessel, and I submit myself to Your Spirit. I will follow You and do whatever You tell me to do.

Thank You for giving me the wisdom and strength to be an excellent worship leader. As You lead me, so I will follow You.

In Jesus' name, amen.

CHAPTER 5

MUSICIANS NEED DYNAMITE

In our study on worship without limits thus far, we've focused on the different elements and requirements needed for the praise and worship leader. While the leader is critical in determining the direction and flow of the worship service, the musicians are key to dynamic worship as well. Without properly executing their gifts, submitting to leadership, and flowing with the Spirit of God, supporting musicians can limit the effectiveness of any given worship service.

Because worship teams are incomplete without all the different members of the group, I'd like to turn my attention in this chapter to the musicians. As integral parts of the worship team, each musician comprises a significant part of the overall worship dynamic. Without the musicians' cooperation and support, the leader cannot do his or her part properly, nor can the Spirit of God flow fully. If you are a musician, know that your part is absolutely necessary!

It's important for you to understand that God has placed you on that stage for a divine purpose. Your purpose is not to be a rock star or to look cool on the platform. Your function is that of a worshipper, and you are to give glory to God in all that you do. Just like the team leader, you are to be a vessel for God's presence to manifest in the people attending the service.

QUALITY AND ANOINTING CREATE DYNAMITE

Regardless of what your position is on the team or what instrument you play, *quality* and the *anointing* are keys to your growth and progress. Without these two spiritual elements present in your life and ministry, you won't be able to fully function at maximum capacity as a worshipper or in any other area of life.

Quality is the practical development and execution of your craft. When you're playing in God's house, you need to bring your best. This means you need to be excellent in all that you do. Don't come to the service unprepared and expect others to pick up your slack. Invest time at home to practice and practice until you become skillful in your craft. Know your music theory and your notes. Commit to the process of growth and development in your musical talents and in your teamwork skills.

You need to be excellent in all that you do. Don't come to the service unprepared and expect others to pick up your slack.

The anointing is the spiritual side to worship. It's the place where the Spirit of God teaches you, instructs you, and leads you in executing your craft. This is when His presence and power come upon you to carry your musical gift into a place where it cannot function on its own or in your own natural abilities.

When fused together, quality and anointing create an explosion in worship. It's the dynamite needed for worship without limits. Combining these two elements is like setting off a Holy Spirit bomb that ministers to the Lord and blesses the people.

When fused together, quality and anointing create an explosion in worship.

I've been in services where there was a lot of quality but no power. The musicians and vocalists were skilled in their craft, but there was no anointing, no presence, and no power. The worship service wasn't any different from a secular concert! The music might have been great, but the spiritual atmosphere was flat. People were not affected in a long-lasting way because the power of God was not present to minister or transform due to the absence of the anointing.

On the other hand, I've also been in services where there was a lot of spiritual hunger. People were crying out to God and worshipping in their hearts, but there was no professionalism at all. Because quality was absent, the music was all over the place.

In either case, the lack of one ingredient impacted the service in a negative way. It takes both quality and anointing to produce effective, transformational worship. And as a musician in the house of God, it is your responsibility to carry both quality and anointing. This is what creates the worship dynamic that ushers in the power of the Holy Spirit.

Interestingly, the word for the power of the Holy Spirit is actually *dunamis,* which means "dynamite." This is the same word used to describe the power of the Holy Spirit that was poured out on the disciples on the day of Pentecost in Acts 2:2. Prior to that event, Jesus gave specific instructions to His followers in Acts 1:8:

> *But **you shall receive power when the Holy Spirit has come upon you;** and you shall be witnesses to Me in Jerusalem, and in all Judea and Samaria, and to the end of the earth.*

The disciples couldn't be effective witnesses for the Lord Jesus without this dynamite power of the Holy Spirit.

Can you imagine how incredible the day of Pentecost was when the disciples first experienced the Holy Spirit in His fullness? About 120 of them were gathered together in one room when suddenly—out of nowhere—the power of the Holy Spirit showed up like a violent rushing wind and tongues of fire! The disciples had never before encountered anything like this. And when the Holy Spirit fell upon them, they began praying in tongues and became such powerful witnesses for Christ that thousands of people turned to the Lord in one day! (See Acts 1:12–Acts 2:4.) That's the same kind of power available for you and for me.

I believe in the power of the Holy Spirit. I believe in praying in the Holy Spirit. It is the fire inside me, and it stirs my faith. Without that power, I wouldn't be able to be an effective witness or worship leader. In fact, it is God's dynamite power that helps me lead worship as the Holy Spirit directs.

This same power is also available to you through the baptism of the Holy Spirit. Just like on the day of Pentecost, you can be filled with the Holy Spirit and brought to another level in your walk with God. You can be empowered to be a witness for Jesus and to lead others more effectively in the Kingdom!

> *When the day of Pentecost had come, they were all together in one place, and suddenly a sound came from heaven like a rushing violent wind, and it filled the whole house where they were sitting. There appeared to them tongues resembling fire, which were being distributed [among them], and they rested on each one of them [as each person received the Holy Spirit]. And they were all filled [that is, diffused throughout their being] with the Holy Spirit and began to speak in other tongues (different languages), as the Spirit was giving them the ability to speak out [clearly and appropriately]* (Acts 2:1-4 Amplified Bible).

Another rock show can't change anyone, but the power of the Holy Spirit will transform lives, heal bodies, and restore souls.

From one worshipper to another, I encourage you to acquaint yourself with the dynamite power inside you through the presence of the Holy Spirit. You need to become familiar with His power so you can help lead others into an atmosphere of God's power. Another rock show can't change anyone, but the power of the Holy Spirit will transform lives, heal bodies, and restore souls. God wants to show forth His power and glory to people, and you can have a part in connecting others to that power if you are a willing and yielded vessel.

So, when you're playing on stage or singing with the people, stay focused on the anointing. You're not on stage to look cool with your fancy musical tricks or to impress people with your stylish leather jacket or ripped jeans. You're on the worship team to bring your quality of musicianship into the house of the Lord and to flow with the Spirit of God. Remember, the show isn't about you or your hip vibe—it's about Jesus and His power and authority.

YOU ARE RESPONSIBLE

If you serve as a supporting musician on your team, your preparation and spiritual sensitivity is important to the entire worship team. Often, people mistakenly think that the worship leader carries the sole responsibility for the direction and effectiveness of the worship service. But that isn't true, nor is it the way it's supposed to be. Each musician and vocalist plays an integral part in the group, because together you are to operate as a team. Individually and corporately, you carry a shared responsibility to prepare with excellence, sharpen your skills, work together in unity, pray, live upright before the Lord, fast, and flow with the Spirit of God in the service. While the worship leader is responsible to lead, the musicians are equally responsible to carry their weight and work together with the rest of the team.

You see, a worship team is a microcosm of the family of God. When you come together as a team, there is a merger of different personalities, abilities, and positions. No one on the team is exactly alike; and in fact, several of you may be completely opposite from one another. Yet, in spite of your differences, you are to care for one another and flow in harmony together. I call this the *Third Rule of Worship: Work Together as a Family.* Each of you bring a special contribution to the whole, and without your contribution, the music wouldn't come out right. Together, you are a spiritual family exemplifying the relational dynamics of the family of God to the whole church.

Together, you are a spiritual family exemplifying the relational dynamics of the family of God to the whole church.

From a presentation standpoint, it looks so much better when everyone is doing their part and operating in the same flow. If the leader is jumping and shouting while the rest of the team is just standing there without any energy or excitement, it presents a pretty poor picture to those in attendance. Honestly, if the worship team doesn't demonstrate unity first, how will the rest of the church begin to come together in one accord in worship? As a team, your unity and teamwork speak volumes to the church. Together, you set the example of how to flow together in the presence of God.

One way to hinder unity on the worship team is by focusing attention on yourself. When you're on the stage thinking about how cool you are, how nervous you may be, or how awesome your voice sounds, you're self-absorbed and self-centered. Remember, worship is not about you; it's about Jesus. You're not the only one on the stage; you're part of the team and a member of the Body of Christ. What you do affects others. So, don't fall for the trap of selfishness—be a team player and a servant leader!

When each member of the team adjusts his or her focus on exalting Jesus and cooperating with one another, the worship will flow to a much deeper and unified place. This team dynamic will even show up in the body language of the musicians. For example, the bass player may exchange glances with the drummer, and both will be enjoying themselves and the sound they're creating together. At the end of a song, all the vocalists and musicians will look at each other and smile when they've hit just that right note.

You see, working together as a team in worship isn't about pride or competition. In fact, those two attitudes will destroy anything God wants to do through you and your colleagues if you allow these attitudes into your team. A worship team is to function just like any other team—each one brings his or her unique supply, and together they produce something far better than what each could produce on their own. Like in a healthy family, the worship team is a safe place where each member's opinion matters and is well respected and celebrated. When the members share familiarity, interaction, encouragement, and celebration, the worship team is poised for success!

A worship team flowing together in harmony and joy not only establishes the right tone in worship for those gathered, but it also affects the nonbelievers who are present in the service. The world can offer all kinds of music and rhythm, but it cannot reproduce the presence of God. So when the worship team actually functions as a team under the direction and unity of the Holy Spirit, God's presence has freedom to flow and minister to the lost. Souls can be impacted for eternity!

CONTRIBUTING OR PREVENTING

At this point, you might be thinking, *Yeah, but I still think the leader is responsible for the worship. I'm just here to play and sing. It doesn't matter if I'm cooperative or competitive. My attitudes and actions don't affect the team or the worship service.* If you think you're not important or that your creativity and cooperation don't matter, you're mistaken. While the leader may carry more responsibility because of his or her leadership position, you are also responsible before God for how you treat the house of God and submit to leadership.

Let me give you an example of this from the Bible. In the book of Joshua, the people of Israel were on a mission to conquer the land of Canaan, the land God had promised them and their descendants. God had already delivered them from the Egyptians, provided manna in the desert, and parted the Jordan River. They were now in the Promised Land taking over one territory after another. These guys were some serious conquistadors!

However, God had laid some ground rules for their conquests. As long as they obeyed God's instructions, they won every battle they encountered. But the moment they disobeyed God's commands, they would lose to their enemies.

Well, one day soon after their victory over the city of Jericho, Joshua and the people of Israel went out to conquer the people of Ai. They had already established an astonishing victory in Jericho, and these guys were pumped about winning again. However, something terrible happened—the Israelites were sorely defeated! As Joshua began to seek God for help, the Lord revealed to him the cause of defeat. One man in Israel had disobeyed God's explicit instructions after the triumph in Jericho, secretly stealing items God had forbidden the people to take. Although only one man had disobeyed the Lord, it affected the whole camp. God saw it all, and this man's secret sin cost the entire nation of Israel to lose the battle! (See Joshua chapters 7 and 8.)

As a member of the worship team, your personal actions and attitudes matter a great deal, and they can either contribute to or prevent the success of your team. Yes, your worship team leader is responsible, just like Joshua was responsible to lead the children of Israel into victory. But you are also responsible to God and to your team for the overall effectiveness of the worship service. If you're not doing your part, you can affect your team's victory just like that one Israelite man did. God expects you to obey just as much as He expects the leadership to obey.

You may be thinking, *We live in the New Testament now. That obedience thing was just something they had to do in the Old Testament.* While we do live under the dispensation of grace, we still have an individual responsibility before God to obey His Word. In fact, our obedience—or lack thereof—has a profound impact on those around us. Allowing sin to take hold in our lives gives place to the devil and destroys our life and ministry.

What makes grace so amazing is that we can repent and change the direction of our actions. Through repentance, we can seek forgiveness from God and from others. As a result, we can have restored fellowship with the Lord and with other believers. Because of the tremendous power unleashed in true repentance and restoration, we can be used by God in a mighty way!

There have been times in my life when I have had to correct attitudes with my team before we are ready to go on stage. Occasionally, there's been a spirit of strife that has tried to come in and divide our team from each other and from the assignment God has given us through worship. So, whenever I start hearing team members start talking unkindly to one another, it's my responsibility as the leader to bring immediate correction. I know that if we allow strife and division to begin expressing itself in our team, the devil will have us beat. We can't lead a congregation into unity and into the presence of God if we're a dysfunctional team ourselves! What we are on the stage and who we are inside is what we bring to the house of God.

Whenever we have team members who won't control their attitudes or behaviors before we lead worship, I'll ask them to sit out that service. Sure, we may have to go without a bass player or a drummer for that day, but it is far more costly to surrender to strife than it is to go without an instrument during a set. I refuse to have a spirit of strife on the stage when God expects us to be examples of unity in His house.

What we are on the stage and who we are inside is what we bring to the house of God.

Unbiblical behavior in leadership isn't just limited to poor attitudes and contention, it also extends to sexual sin as well. Adultery, homosexuality, pornography, and sex before marriage should not be tolerated on the worship team, because they are sinful actions condemned in Scripture. Believers are to refrain themselves from these sins and traps, and leadership is held to an even higher standard of accountability and purity. If someone on the worship team is actively sinning and does not want to change, they should not be allowed to bring that standard into God's house.

When we close our eyes to sin, we are no different from the world and become a powerless church. Many times we make excuses like, "I know he's in sin, but I'm going to let it pass because he's such a good musician, and we need him!" However, God's Word tells us this kind of thinking is wrong (see Micah 3:4 Amplified Bible). We can never allow talent to be praised over character. That is exactly what the world does, and we cannot reflect God's light and be like the world at the same time (Matthew 5:13-16 NIV).

REPENTING OF PRIVATE SIN

The issue of obedience and cooperation go much further than just poor attitudes like laziness, self-centeredness, pride, or competition. It also pertains to your personal life outside of the church walls. You may think no one minds if you're sleeping around with your girlfriend on the side, watching porn, lying to your boss, or gossiping about others. But I'm warning you—God sees it. He sees it all. And what you do behind closed doors will come out in the open if you refuse to repent.

The issue of obedience and cooperation go much further than just poor attitudes.

Perhaps this truth bomb may sound a bit harsh, but I'm saying this to you in a spirit of love to help you, not to judge you. Since none of us are immune to temptations and failures, all of us need the power of the Holy Spirit to withstand sin. Sadly, many have had incredible promise in ministry, but because they allowed sin to have place in their lives, they never fulfilled their purpose and calling.

I don't want to see the same heartbreaking story happen to you. As your brother in the Lord, I'm cheering you on to the finish line! And if that means I have to get in your face with some truth bombs to help you reach your destiny in Christ, then that's what I'll do. More than anything, I desire God's highest and best for you!

For you to finish your course, it's critical you understand how dangerous sin is to your personal life, your calling, and your ministry. Your private sin will always—and I do mean always—affect your public life. So, if you're dealing with issues in your personal life but still worshipping God on the platform with the worship team, you need to deal with the sin first because it doesn't affect just you. Sin affects the whole team, no matter who it is or if it's hidden or public. No sin is private in the eyes of God.

If you are struggling with sin and have attempted to hide it from others, you need to talk to your spiritual leader today! Not only will a good leader chastise you in love, but he or she will also push you forward to your destiny in Christ. You may need to step down from leadership for a while, but when you come back, you'll be stronger and more anointed than you ever were. Whatever issue may be troubling you, please don't procrastinate in getting help from the Body of Christ. What is hidden will always be revealed. It's much better for you to honestly confront sin than to keep hiding it until it comes out in the open, bringing along with it much shame and hurt. You can be free!

I want to encourage you right now that if you're dealing with sin in any part of your life to stop right now and repent. God's grace and mercy are available to you if you will receive them. The Bible tells us God is faithful and just to forgive us and to cleanse us from all unrighteousness (1 John 1:9). No matter what you've done, the blood of Jesus can cleanse you and make you whole. He can wash away all the guilt and stain of sin!

After you've confessed your sin to God and repented of it, you also need to remove yourself from temptation. If you've been gossiping about people to your friends, keep your mouth shut the next time you're tempted to say something ugly about others. If you've been struggling in the areas of sexual purity, immediately remove yourself from the tempting situation. Go to a trusted, godly friend and ask him or her to be your accountability partner. Whatever actions you need to do to stay free from sin, do it! Don't delay.

Next, you must feed your spirit in this area of weakness. For example, if you have problems controlling your temper, find Scriptures and teachings about self-control, dealing with your anger, and guarding your mouth. If you've been struggling in the area of physical purity, find out what God says in His Word about presenting your body as a living sacrifice and replacing fleshly lust with true love. Your body is the temple of the Holy Spirit, and what you do with it matters greatly to the Lord.

Finally, look for doors that you've opened to that temptation in the first place. Sometimes, the movies and music we listen to or the friends we hang out with subtly take us away from God and His standards of holiness. I encourage you to examine what you've been feeding your mind and your flesh. Are the songs you're listening to exalting things God specifically warns against in His Word? What about the TV shows you're watching? Are they suggestive, full of foul language, or violent? Then turn them off! Give the devil no place in your life to trip you up anymore.

OVERCOMING ADDICTIONS AND STRONGHOLDS

Throughout Scripture, we see that God has already provided a way out of sin. Whenever you begin to think your situation is hopeless, just remember God has given you His Word, the blood of Jesus, and the power of the Holy Spirit. By His grace, you can overcome all sin and live a holy life. Holiness is not out of your reach, and you're not a "special case." If you're born again, you have equal access to God's purity and power just like any other believer. It's up to you to do something with what God has already given you.

Not only do you need to be honest with yourself about the sin, but you also need to face the problem head-on in complete transparency with the Lord and with those who are being affected by your sin.

If you've struggled with an area in your life beyond normal temptation, and you can't seem to get the victory, the first step is to be honest with yourself about the problem. Constantly battling the same issue over and over is usually a sign of an addiction or stronghold in your life. This particular area of bondage needs to be dealt with in an honest and straightforward manner. Not only do you need to be honest with yourself about the sin, but you also need to face the problem head-on in complete transparency with the Lord and with those who are being affected by your sin. The Bible says in First John 1:9, *"If we confess our sins, He is faithful and just to forgive us our sins and to cleanse us from all unrighteousness."* Note that confession—or honesty about the sin—is a requirement for freedom from that sin.

To overcome an addiction, you also need to take serious steps to renew your mind. Romans 12:2 (NIV) says, *"Do not conform to the pattern of this world, but be transformed by the renewing of your mind. Then you will be able to test and approve what God's will is—his good, pleasing and perfect will."* Renewing your mind means daily meditating, studying, and reading the Bible. When battling addictions, you need to be equipped to fight the devil and your own flesh with truth from God's Word.

DO THE BIBLE

When reading your Bible, look for Scriptures that specifically deal with your particular issue, provide the solution to the problem, show you your victory in Christ, and teach you how to live like a true disciple of Jesus. Then you must put that Word into practice. Don't just *read* the Bible, *do* the Bible! Your life of discipline to apply the Word is key to victorious Christian living.

Don't just *read* the Bible, *do* the Bible!

For example, you may be trying to overcome an addiction to pornography, and you know God's Word says to flee from youthful lusts (2 Timothy 2:22). So what do you do the next time you're sitting alone with a computer and you're tempted to click on a website that promotes lust? Do you linger at the computer—or do you jump up, turn the computer off and run out of the room? If you're being a doer of the Word and serious about overcoming that addiction, you're going to do everything you can to flee a tempting situation. And if that means you have to completely unplug your computer and put it in storage for a few months until you have broken free from that porn addiction, then you do it! By allowing yourself to be governed by the Word of God, you will overcome every addiction and stronghold that has held you back in your walk with Christ.

Another key to victory is to invite the Holy Spirit into your life to empower you in a supernatural way. As a believer, you need God's power in your life to be a witness and to live a godly life in an ungodly world. This supernatural power comes through the infilling of the Holy Spirit with the evidence of speaking in tongues. Not only does being filled with Holy Spirit give you the spiritual fortitude needed to overcome difficulties, but praying every day in tongues strengthens your spirit. (See Jude verses 19-25.) The Holy Spirit is a powerful promise from the Father for every believer in Christ.

Finally, overcoming addictions is not possible without true humility. If you've struggled for years trying to justify or hide sinful behavior, it's time for you to humble yourself and ask for help. You may even need to seek counseling from a pastor, a treatment center, or a professional Christian counselor. When seeking help, be sure to find someone who is trustworthy and who can give you Bible-based counsel. You need to be completely transparent with this person; don't be afraid to be open and honest with your struggles. James 5:16 (NIV) says, *"Therefore confess your sins to each other and pray for each other so that you may be healed...."* Humility before God and others in addressing your problems can be the very key that unlocks your prison door.

Overcoming addictions is not possible without true humility.

As a side note, I recommend considering such programs like Celebrate Recovery, a Bible-based discipleship program committed to helping people overcome addictions. Another great resource is *Battlefield of the Mind by* Joyce Meyer. God's love and grace is available to bring you total freedom, but it's up to you to take steps of action, obedience, and faith. If you do what's required to deal honestly with your issues, God will help you supernaturally overcome any and every addiction that has held you captive. Sin doesn't have to keep you bound anymore—you can live free!

UNITY: A PRECURSOR TO THE MIRACULOUS

Being liberated from hidden sins, strongholds, and addictions will not only affect your mind, your emotions, and your quality of life, it will also impact everyone around you, which includes your family, loved ones, friends, and band members. In fact, your freedom will completely change the way you flow together as a band and how you are able to minister to others through your gift of music.

This is another reason why it's important to be honest with your team and your pastor. As mentioned previously, a worship team is like a family. The more we work together, the stronger we are in carrying out our assignment. It's important for us to pray together as a team, to cry out together as a team, to read our Bibles together as a team, and to even repent as a team.

There is no big "I" and little "you" in the Body of Christ—we're in this thing together, each rowing our own paddle to move us together to the other side. And when we work together as a team, we create an atmosphere for God to do miraculous things in our midst. Unity is a precursor to the miraculous!

So, remember that no matter what your place is on the worship team—the team lead, a musician, or a singer—you affect the overall success of the team. If you're carrying an offense toward another person, it's tangible in the atmosphere and on the stage. Your worship team is like your family, and whatever is going on in the family will affect how well you play together as musicians and how powerful your worship will be together as believers. Nothing can remain hidden forever, and you can rest assured that all things will eventually come to light. So be quick to repent, quick to forgive, and quick to walk in love!

My friend, you are such a vital member on your worship team and in the Body of Christ. You can either contribute to the building of God's house through your preparation, spirit of excellence, godly behaviors and attitudes, and holy lifestyle—or you can prevent God's people from moving forward due to laziness, pride, selfishness, competition, strife, and lack of purity. The choice to activate God's supernatural dynamite is yours today. If you commit to doing your part and submitting to the Spirit of God, you can bring an invaluable measure of power to your team, your pastor, and your church!

PRAYER

Father God, I ask You for forgiveness. I repent for any laziness, selfishness, pride, competition, or strife that may have cropped up in my life.

Lord, I understand that any personal addictions I may be struggling with affect the whole team as well as the quality of our worship. Lord, I repent right now of (name sin here). Your Word says that You are faithful and just to forgive me of all sins and to cleanse me from unrighteousness. So, Lord, I receive Your forgiveness. Thank You for washing me clean in the blood of Jesus. I commit from this day forward to remove myself from temptation, to feed my spirit, and to keep the door closed on the devil.

Lord, I also ask You to fill me with Your Holy Spirit. I thank You that the infilling of the Holy Spirit is a promise from Father God to all believers. I receive Your power right now with the evidence of speaking in tongues. Thank You for the Holy Spirit who gives me boldness to be a witness and empowers me to live upright before You in a clean and pure way!

Lord, I take up my responsibility to lead a life of purity before You both on and off the stage. I want to be a team player. I want to encourage others on my team as we seek Your face and Your will for our lives. I commit to staying free from strife and envy; I will be a person who contributes to the success of my team instead of preventing it.

Today, I make a commitment in my heart to be a person of purity and humility before You, heavenly Father. I will do my best to prepare and cultivate my craft. This is a gift You gave me, and I want to glorify and honor You in all that I do. As I surrender to You, I thank You for anointing me to play in the house of God. Because I am cooperating with You, with my leadership, and with my team, we will see You move miraculously in our midst! Thank You so much for Your presence and Your power today.

In Jesus' name, amen.

CHAPTER 6

MELODY AND KEY BRING UNITY

As previously noted, any excellent worship team or leader needs to develop both spiritual and natural disciplines in order to facilitate transformational worship. While the spiritual elements remain the most critical, it is still important to execute exceptional craftsmanship in our music. God has invested in us various musical talents and abilities, and He expects us to be good stewards of those graces: *"Each of you should use whatever gift you have received to serve others, as faithful stewards of God's grace in its various forms"* (1 Peter 4:10 NIV). To be anything less is to be an unfaithful steward of the gifts and callings of God.

Of course, there are a myriad of practical tips I could share about stewarding your gift and sharpening your skills, but I'd like to bring your attention to something extremely pragmatic that many church musicians overlook. This is a simple but integral principle for successful worship: melody and key bring unity. Let me explain.

When writing a song, the composer is generally thinking about the sound, the rhythm, the notes, and the arrangement. But when writing a song that's to be sung by the public in a group setting, the composer is also concerned with how easy the composition is for others to sing. If the arrangement is too complicated for others to reproduce vocally, then the usefulness of the song will remain limited.

As worship songwriters and composers, it's important for us to remember we are not arranging the melodies just for ourselves—we are creating music that others can sing in worship to God. If we keep this precept in mind, we will bring both excellence and unity to every song we write, produce, sing, and direct.

UNITY IN SIMPLICITY

Now I'm not saying you should write elementary or rudimentary songs. In fact, you can and should let your creativity flourish! However, you must keep the melodies simple enough for corporate singing. If the melody is catchy and easy for the general public to sing, then you have faithfully stewarded your gift as a worship leader and songwriter.

A simple test of a great worship melody is how quickly people can repeat a song after they've heard it.

A simple test of a great worship melody is how quickly people can repeat a song after they've heard it. Generally, someone should be able to sing a melody thirty seconds after being heard for the first time. So when you're arranging the worship chords, be sure the congregation can catch the melody when you present a song. If they have trouble singing along, then the melody is too complicated for group singing. And if the people assembled can't sing together, then all you have is a concert, not worship.

Remember, one of our purposes as worship leaders is to bring people together in unity as we enter the Lord's presence together. Another way of promoting that unity is by presenting songs that we all can sing together. Sure, the vocalists on stage may be able to belt out that one particularly difficult song, but what about those who are not gifted musically? For the most part, a typical congregation will have only a few musicians represented. Therefore, in order for everyone to flow together in song, we must choose melodies that the average person can easily sing.

Another thing to remember is that if we're presenting songs that are too complicated for congregational singing, people will end up watching instead of participating. And do you know what that is? A concert. It's not worship. Remember, we are worshippers not performers. In our pursuit of worship without limits, we must keep this truth grounded in our hearts at all times. We are worshippers giving glory to God, not performers glorying in the attention of others.

Remember, we are worshippers not performers.

An example of an excellent worship songwriter is Chris Tomlin. I love and respect his gift in the Body of Christ very much. Notice how beautiful his songwriting style and composition is while remaining transferable to congregational singing. Everyone knows his songs, and churches everywhere have reproduced his songs in services for years. Songs like "How Great Is Our God" are catchy, simple, and memorable enough for anyone to sing anytime, anywhere. His simplicity in songwriting and arrangement have blessed the Church all around the world!

So when you are practicing songs with your band, remember to keep the melodies simple. Your songs shouldn't be stale or lacking in creativity, but they should be easy enough for all to sing. Stick to songs that can be sung by all—young and old, men and the women, the musically gifted and the musically challenged. By implementing this one simple principle, you will be one step closer to establishing unmistakable unity between the musicians and the congregation and between the older generation and the younger. Melody is key in establishing unity!

You can see this principle at work in the world's music. When you hear a song on the radio, you're not singing the drum beat—you are singing the hook in the melody! Again, the way melody works in the Church is no different. Sadly, the devil learned this skill in Heaven and perverted it to use in the world. But if Christians learn this secret of melody, we can reclaim its power and bring people together in unity for Jesus!

UNITY IN PRIORITY

One of the elements that make music anywhere pop is the instrumentation. Like all musicians, I enjoy good arrangements. I love it when the drums are loud, the guitars are cranking, or little computer sounds are echoing in the background. However, if all the instrumentation is louder than the melody, then there's a problem, especially in a corporate worship setting.

From a musical standpoint, one of the most important things we need to hear is the melody, but we also need to hear the words. When the instruments overpower the lyrics, then people can't focus on what they are singing. The words are the first priority in corporate worship, because they are built upon the principles of the Bible. By drowning out the words through an overemphasis on sound or instrumentation, we greatly hinder the effectiveness of worship.

The words are the first priority in corporate worship, because they are built upon the principles of the Bible.

Ultimately, a poor mixing of sound and style ignores what is most important in corporate worship. The melody and words bring life from the Bible and unite the congregation. When people are joining together in worship, they've stopped thinking about the math exam at school the next day, the sick kids at home, or the overdue bills. Rather, they are focused on one thing and one thing alone—Jesus!

UNITY IN VOICE

In addition to creating the right melody, we must also be cognizant of presenting the song in the right key. Like the melody, the key of the song has to be something everyone in the congregation can sing regardless of age or gender. For example, if a key is too high, it will be difficult for men to sing, and if a key is too low, it will be difficult for women to sing. Again, our purpose is to establish corporate unity as we worship the Lord.

When I write my songs, I keep in mind that others may not be able to sing them as comfortably as I can. So, I let others try to sing them before we officially make them part of our worship set. If the key is too strenuous for either the men or women, then I'll adjust the key a half-step or two.

Of course, not all the key changes are the perfect fit for me personally. But I've learned that leading a worship band or service is not about me! What's more important than my personal comfort is the opportunity for unity. This is what I call the *Fourth Rule of Worship: Put Others First Regarding Melody and Unity.* If it's easier for more people to sing in one key than another, I set the song where it benefits the majority. This teamwork facilitates a time when we can all enter into worship together and lift up our voices to God. The greatest sound on earth is when God's people are crying out to Him together in one accord!

UNITY IN HUMILITY

Finally, each of us needs to remember that worship is not about us; it's about glorifying God and unifying His people. As musicians, it's imperative we cultivate this one, very critical habit—learn to think about others. I know it's tempting to always be concerned with how my voice sounds, how that key suits me, or how that arrangements fits my style. But it's not about me. It's about presenting to God a beautiful sacrifice of worship from His people.

If I'm the only one shining, then I'm not doing my job correctly.

Over the years, I've learned to humble myself before God and with the other musicians. If I'm the only one shining, then I'm not doing my job correctly. Since my purpose is to facilitate unity in worship and glorify God, then I must always put God and others first. By remaining humble in this area, I've seen the Lord move in powerful ways when I lead worship. It's amazing how humility opens the door to God's manifested presence and power!

Let me share an example of this from my own life from just a few years ago. In 2013, I was traveling to the United States for a music festival and tour. Because I grew up as a missionary kid, I hadn't lived in the US since I was six and had only returned for our yearly family visits. I had never before shared my music in the States, and so this was an especially exciting time for me.

During that time, my band and I were invited to co-headline a festival near Nashville, the heart of the Christian music industry. In Russia, we have large Christian events, but we don't have as many styles of Christian music represented as in the US. I was excited to hear so many different genres and artists come together to represent Christ at one time!

My team had developed a great bond of unity from spending so much time together on the road. We also had learned to pray with one another before every event. Personally, I believe prayer is key to humility that opens the door to unity and revival.

Personally, I believe prayer is key to humility that opens the door to unity and revival.

During the festival, I invited Jeff, one of the promoters, to come pray with us. I had met Jeff a year before when he was working at Salem Radio / *CCM Magazine* and attending Charis Bible College in Colorado. Jeff loved the ministry we were doing in missions and music and had a great heart for orphans in Eastern Europe. Little did I know at the time that Jeff had also been hurt and disappointed from his experience working in the music industry. But on the day we invited him to pray with us and our team, the Holy Spirit began a new work in his heart. He would say that he was not really a worshipper. Music was a past idol of unmet dreams and God needed to deliver him from this disappointment of artists and music industry letdowns that blocked his ability to worship.

It was a simple thing of asking him to pray with us hours before our stage time, but it disarmed him. At this festival there were open fields around us, and we walked to a secluded area, got on our knees, raised our hands, and started praying in the Holy Spirit. We were living what I call worship *Rule 8: Must have a demonstration of your walk with God, on and off the stage.*

Jeff said he was not really a worshipper, he would engage, but was more waiting for it to be over so he could hear the Word preached and taught. This was a serious wall—a dangerous area to have truth, but not the spirit of worship and praise in your heart. From that moment of prayer, he told me that he was disarmed to receive, and the process of healing and restoration that lifted rejection, disappointment, and unrealized dreams from his life had started. Jeff encouraged his family to attend our worship concert that night and the Holy Spirit started stripping off the layers of hardness. The next morning, my Renner Worship team had a morning session of worship and I spoke to festival attendees.

God not only touched Jeff, but also his wife heard God speak clearly to her heart about their special-needs daughter and how God loved her and would use her. Their daughter, Leeza, at the time was age eight, and during morning worship received a supernatural gift of prayer, she raised her hands and started worshipping! Leeza had been adopted from Ukraine and the mother drank vodka while she was pregnant. It was hard for her to speak full sentences and put words together. But when she prays, she is articulate, powerful, and can bring down Heaven! God is so good.

From that day forward, Jeff and his entire family were changed and set free. Through our simple act of openness, humility, unity, and prayer, the Holy Spirit was able to touch someone's life and bring much needed healing. That's the power of unity in humility!

In addition to Jeff's testimony, God's power through unity was released that day throughout the different bands that came together. Regardless of denomination or musical style, the musicians, leaders, and attendees all flowed together in unity during the festival. People were praying for one another freely and spontaneously. The Holy Spirit moved in such an amazing way among His people! And it was all because unity and humility were present in the hearts of those who gathered together in Christ's name during a Christian music festival in Nashville.

When we consider how others are affected, not only by how we live our lives but also by our choices in style, key, and arrangement, we are actually walking in love as Scripture commands. And do you know what the Bible says about that? It says that perfect love casts out all fear! (See First John 4:18.) By considering others and walking in love—even in simple things like adjusting keys to a comfortable range for everyone—we give God the opportunity to demonstrate Himself in our midst. We create an atmosphere where fear is absent and love is present.

This type of dynamic atmosphere is palpable to all, especially those who are not part of the family of God. When nonbelievers come into a church service and observe everyone singing together in unity, anointing, and power, you can guarantee they will want to know more about this Jesus! As people run to the altars to give their hearts to the Lord, we can rejoice knowing we were part of reaching that harvest.

In our role as worship leaders, everything we do has the potential to create an atmosphere for God to move in people's hearts. Even simple, practical things like arranging the right melodies and keys play important roles in cultivating a dynamic spiritual atmosphere. The more we prepare ourselves and yield to the Holy Spirit, the more room we give to the Lord to use our gifts and talents for His glory. By arranging songs with simple melodies and comfortable keys so that everyone can easily enter into worship, we are not only stewarding our gifts and talents well, but we are also connecting others to the presence of God. What a powerful calling!

In our role as worship leaders, everything we do has the potential to create an atmosphere for God to move in people's hearts.

PRAYER

Father God, I ask You to help me in arranging the songs we use for worship. Help me to choose the right key and melody so that all can benefit from this time in Your presence. I desire to be a vessel used by You to bring unity among Your people in worship through simplicity, priority, voice, and humility.

Lord, I ask You for songs from Heaven. Fill my mouth with Your words and anoint me to write and compose music that glorifies You. I thank You that our melodies are going to originate from Heaven itself and that our keys will be perfect. Together, we're going to enter into Your presence and see Your power demonstrated in our midst.

I pray this in Jesus' name, amen.

CHAPTER 7

CONNECTION ON STAGE

Have you ever been in a conversation with someone and the person's eyes were on everything else except you? It's pretty frustrating, isn't it? When you're talking to someone, you expect attention and connection. Without that appropriate focus and eye contact, you don't know if you're being heard or understood correctly by the other person.

As leaders on the stage, we have to keep our eyes open to connect properly with our team, the pastor, and the people.

Well, this same principle holds true in public worship. In fact, I like to call this the *Fifth Rule of Worship: Maintain Eye Contact.* As leaders on the stage, we have to keep our eyes open to connect properly with our team, the pastor, and the people. While it's perfectly fine to worship with our eyes closed at home, this habit actually limits our effectiveness in public leadership.

I know it may sound so simple—and even a little absurd—but don't worship on the stage with your eyes closed. Keep them open when you're leading worship! That said, if you're working with your pastor, and he or she asks for every eye to be closed, please follow this admonishment. Especially during times when an altar call is given, it's appropriate to close your eyes in reverence and respect.

Other than specific times of congregational prayer, when you go off into your own little world and start worshipping on your own with your eyes closed, you may be enjoying alone time with Jesus. However, it's not helping to lead the Body effectively in a public worship setting. Of course, when you're at home in your own quiet time, you can worship Jesus all by yourself and keep your eyes closed the whole time if you want. That's your special time with the Lord. But when you're on the stage, God expects you to assist Him in leading others into His presence; therefore, your priority shifts. This time on the stage is not about just you and Jesus—it's about leading others into a place of corporate intimacy with the Lord.

PROMOTING UNITY

First, by keeping your eyes open during worship, you are establishing an open awareness of others and creating a valuable point of connection with those around you, especially with the congregation. As you're leading and making eye contact with different people in the room, you are telling them, "I see you. I'm real just like you. God loves you and He cares about you."

Not only will this critical action allow others to connect with you during worship, but it will also open doors for ministry.

Making eye contact with the congregation will reinforce the truth you're singing and help others grab hold of that truth as well. By establishing that connection, you're speaking forth the things of God directly to them so that it can penetrate their hearts.

As a side note, eye contact is also extremely important for everyone watching the service online. When you're in the auditorium, you may miss what people do or don't do, but when you're watching online, you can see everything! Every detail stands out. So when you close your eyes on stage, online viewers will see things completely differently, and it won't look right to them. They may have been connecting to you during worship, but the moment you close your eyes, they become disconnected.

Eye contact is the vehicle for connection and communication in worship, just as it is in any relationship.

Eye contact is the vehicle for connection and communication in worship, just as it is in any relationship. For example, when a husband and wife speak their love to one another, rarely will they do it with their eyes closed. That would be silly! Usually, they look straight into each other's eyes and speak words from the heart. And when they say, "I love you" with their eyes as well as with their words, it sends a clear message of love to each other.

Now I understand some people may be offended when I point out the obvious in maintaining eye contact, but it is an essential point of connection and communication with others. You can close your eyes all you want at home, but when you are at church on the stage, your eyes are the way you preach Jesus to others, so let them shine!

Let me ask you a question—have you ever seen a pastor close his or her eyes when delivering the message? Of course not! Why? Because the connection with the people would completely be lost.

Maintaining eye contact for the sake of connection is a simple but profound truth. Even in secular concerts, artists never close their eyes when the camera is on them. They remain focused on the audience and sing to the people watching on camera. Again, this a natural communication principle that governs music and connection. The devil knows this stuff, and he has perverted it for the world. We as Christians can and should be wise in our own communication and connection so that Jesus may be glorified!

Second, keeping your eyes open during worship is key for connection with your team. While your band is on the stage, you need to look at each other and nod to one another. These nonverbal cues maintain open lines of communication even when words are not possible. They also demonstrate the family-like care and concern between you and your team. In a small but powerful way, how you handle nonverbal cues exemplifies to others how God's family works together and honors one another.

For example, if you become isolated in your worship and lose connection with your team, you may forget about the order of the songs, the chord changes, or even the words to the music. You won't know what's going on because you disconnected yourself through lack of eye contact. And that disconnection will break the unity every single time.

I realize this is an extremely practical point, but keeping your eyes open is critical to cultivating unity in worship. When you're at home in your personal time with the Lord, it doesn't matter if you're lost in worship or not. But when you're leading worship in a public setting, you are part of a team. And in order for a team to function properly, it must have unity.

Your team needs to see you and needs to know where you are. They need to know you're watching and that you're following the cues from the drummer and other key musicians. In order to preserve the unity and be effective in your time of leading worship, you must keep your eyes open!

SUBMITTING TO AUTHORITY

Finally, eye contact is important for communicating with the pastor or other persons in charge of leading the service. There may be certain times when the pastor will want to step in and speak by the inspiration of the Holy Spirit or may sense the anointing on one particular song and want to continue flowing with it. The pastor may also be led by the Spirit and ask you to go into a completely different song that isn't even on the song list. If you have your eyes closed, you will have no idea what the pastor is doing or what is to be done next. Therefore, your sensitivity and willingness to stay in visual connection with your pastor is critical to the success of any worship service.

Your sensitivity and willingness to stay in visual connection with your pastor is critical to the success of any worship service.

When I was about seventeen, I learned this lesson the hard way when I was leading worship for my father. During one service, I was so moved by the music and the worship that I just closed my eyes and drowned out everything else. I lost connection with the congregation, with my team, and most importantly, with my dad—who was the pastor and senior leadership of that service.

I was so lost in my own world that the musicians didn't know if I was on the chorus or the verse or the bridge. It was total chaos, but I didn't care. My eyes were closed, and I was just enjoying my time with God. I had completely forgotten about the clock—or anyone else for that matter!

During this whole time, my dad was looking at me, trying to give me cues. He was endeavoring to communicate that he was ready to come up on the stage and preach. But I was so out of touch and oblivious to everything else around me—all I was focused on was how much I was enjoying worshipping Jesus.

Suddenly, I felt a tap on my shoulder. My dad was standing next to me and whispered in my ear, "Philip, thank you for worship. I only have fifteen minutes to preach." I felt so bad! He then told me, "Philip, next time you're leading worship, look at me. You have to make eye contact with me."

Despite my embarrassment, I learned a valuable lesson that day. I will never again close my eyes and go into my own world when I'm leading worship because it's selfish. I might have been enjoying my time with the Lord, but I was only thinking of myself. I wasn't thinking about my dad, his authority, the needs of my team members, or even the time allotted for the service. I was just consumed with how much I was enjoying that moment. That's great when I'm at home in my own time with the Lord, but that is not appropriate for servant leadership.

So, learn from my mistake and don't let that happen to you! Keep your eyes open during worship, stay connected with the audience, be in communication with your team, and read the cues from your pastor.

If you lead with your eyes open, I promise it will help strengthen your leadership tremendously! You'll promote unity among the people, bolster teamwork with your band, and maintain cooperation with your pastor. By following this one simple technique, the worship experience in your church will advance another level into that place of God's limitless power and presence.

PRAYER

Father God, I thank You for teaching me how to flow with Your Spirit during times of worship. I commit to follow You, submit to authority, and grow into an outstanding worship leader.

Thank You for teaching me even the practical aspects of leadership so that I can be a blessing to my pastor, my church, and my team. Help me to remember to lead with my eyes open, making contact with others as we worship You together. I thank You for unity in the congregation, for harmony with our band, and for open lines of communication with those in authority. I pray for a heightened sense of awareness and sensitivity as we all flow together with Your Spirit in worship.

Thank You for helping me raise the bar in worship and to become an excellent steward of my calling. I refuse to allow selfishness to rule in me; I commit to being a humble servant leader who glorifies You in all that I do. I love You, Lord Jesus!

In Jesus' name, amen.

CHAPTER 8

NO LIMITS WITH THE HOLY SPIRIT

As you pursue worship without limits, keep in mind that this is a lifestyle of growth. It's not an event but a process that requires consistent application and progress. Some of what we've discussed in this book will be easy for you to implement right away; other things will take time for you to develop as you grow in your walk with the Lord, in your leadership and musical abilities, and in those deep places of worship. Whatever it takes for you to encounter that flow of transformational worship, I encourage you to do it!

Above all, it's important you give the Holy Spirit proper place in your life and in your times of worship. As mentioned before, limitless worship is activated when both the anointing and quality are fused together. It explodes when the Holy Spirit is leading it.

When you allow the Holy Spirit to direct your times of worship, something truly powerful takes place. Miracles happen, the gifts of the Spirit are manifested, the peace of God rains down, and the atmosphere becomes thick with His presence. This is the pivot point that elevates worship to another level. But it can't happen unless you are willing to cooperate with the Spirit of God.

CHOOSING HIS PLANS INSTEAD OF OURS

Following the Holy Spirit will almost always require you to change your previous plans. You may have already decided that certain songs, a set list, or specific keys will be part of a particular worship session. But on occasion, the Holy Spirit will move in such a way and lead the worship in an entirely different direction from what you or your team had previously planned. When this happens, you have a choice either to hold tight to your plans or to let go and follow God's plans in faith.

As a worship leader, you have the authority to go with your own thing or to submit to the will of God and allow the Holy Spirit to do His thing. Of course, if you remain stubborn and unchanging in your plans, you will forfeit God's anointing and power on that service. God only anoints *His* plans, not human plans!

God only anoints *His* plans, not human plans!

If your heart is to see people's lives and hearts transformed by the power of God, then it's critical to stay sensitive to the Holy Spirit and to the way He is leading during the worship time. Whenever God begins to change the direction of a service, remember He is doing so for a reason. There are certain people He may want to minister to, specific things He may want to say, or a particular truth He may want to get across. If you are willing to flow with Him and be obedient to His leading, you'll be surprised at all He will accomplish during worship. By moving out of the way and allowing the Holy Spirit to do His thing, you and all the people in the church will be tremendously blessed!

Of course, submitting to the leading of the Holy Spirit requires being flexible while relinquishing personal pride. I remember learning this lesson one time during a particular worship service. My team and I had come prepared with a specific list of songs and keys. We had worked really hard, and I was so proud of the flow and sound. Each song built upon the next, and I just knew it was going to be awesome!

Well, about three songs into our set, I heard God whisper to me, "You think you're doing pretty good, don't you?" I was like, "Yeah! I do. I mean this sounds great and we're all playing just fine." Then the Lord said, "But nobody is entering in, are they?" And it was true. We all sounded great, but no one was really entering into worship.

Then the Lord spoke something to my heart I'll never forget. He said, "Philip, you can do this your way and your plan will be fulfilled, or you can do it My way and My will plan will be fulfilled." Well, that was enough for me. I humbled myself, put aside my agenda, and followed the leading of the Holy Spirit. The service went in a completely different direction from what we had planned; we changed the set to songs everyone knew. And do you know whose plans were accomplished that service? God's. He's the One who was glorified, and He's the One whose name was lifted high.

As a worship leader, you may experience times like I did when the Lord will ask you to change your song set in the middle of a service. It may not make sense to you, but you need to be obedient and follow God. Just put down your pride and submit your will to His. If you do that, God will use your willingness to accomplish His plans and fulfill His purpose.

RECOGNIZING THE EBBS AND FLOWS

During times of worship, it's also important for you to recognize the ebbs and flows of worship, or the way in which God is moving or desiring people to respond to Him. Sometimes, the worship may rise to a crescendo of praise where people are shouting and magnifying Jesus. Other times, the worship may reach a deep flow of reverence where a holy hush settles over everyone. As the leader, it's your job to be cognizant of these various veins of worship and to be sensitive to the direction of the Lord.

For example, when the worship reaches a point of depth and reverence, the Lord may even speak to your heart to stop all music for a while and just remain silent in His presence. Those times of stillness in the presence of God are powerful and life changing! In fact, when we sit still and be quiet, it's usually because we're listening to someone else speak. The same principle works in the realm of worship—when the Holy Spirit begins to lead in a vein of silent reverence, He is desiring to speak to people's hearts in that moment of quiet. However, if you fail to yield to that nudge and keep talking or playing, you'll miss what God wants to say to His people.

Have you ever been in a discussion with someone who just continued to talk and talk and talk while never allowing you an opportunity to speak? After a while, you can feel pretty frustrated and unwanted because that person is dominating the entire conversation. Worship follows a similar principle—sometimes God wants us to just sit still and listen to Him speak.

Whenever God speaks to us, our lives are transformed in one way or another. Sometimes it's just as simple as having a fresh understanding of His Person or of a particular truth in His Word. Other times, He speaks to us about the personal details of our lives and how we need to change in an area. Many times, during those quiet times of listening to Him, He gives us direction, wisdom, or answers to the issues we face. No matter what His Spirit speaks to our hearts, every single moment in God's presence is a time of transformation!

No matter what His Spirit speaks to our hearts, every single moment in God's presence is a time of transformation!

When the Holy Spirit leads you into those deeper, quieter times of worship, remember to keep yourself open to what He wants to say in that moment. Ask Him if there's a word He wants you to give out, or if He wants to move in the demonstration of the gifts of the Spirit. For example, God may give you a word of a knowledge about someone present in the audience. When you feel that knowing rising up in your spirit, be bold and speak it out, because God wants to show Himself off! He wants to demonstrate His healing and delivering power right there in the middle of worship.

MOVING IN THE GIFTS OF THE SPIRIT

Following the Holy Spirit and moving in the gifts of the Spirit may be a bit uncomfortable at first, simply because you may not want to embarrass yourself if you miss it. However, as you learn to discern the Holy Spirit's voice and flow in those gifts regularly, you will become more and more comfortable in speaking out what the Holy Spirit shows you. I encourage you to be bold and step out when you sense the Lord is speaking to you. The word He gives you to minister may change someone's life, release the healing power of God, or be the answer to someone's prayer.

I remember leading worship one time in Belarus when the Holy Spirit began moving through me in the gifts of healing. Because my team and I were ministering in a more traditional church, I really didn't want to step out and move in this way. However, during worship, the Holy Spirit gave me a word of knowledge about someone's leg. At that moment, I knew I could either go my own way with my own plans, or I could obey God and follow His plan. So very respectfully, I just said, "You know, there's someone here who has a problem with their leg. God wants to heal you tonight."

What's interesting is when the Lord moved on my heart to give that word out, we were right in the middle of a song where I was supposed to belt out the bridge. I was about to sing, "You, O Lord, are compassionate and gracious, For You, O Lord, are abounding in love." The spotlight was on me, and it was supposed to be my great moment. But God chose that instant to speak to my heart about someone else...about something He wanted to do for someone else. So instead of focusing on me and my plans and my performance, I yielded my will to God and I obeyed.

I spoke that word out just as He instructed. I know God moved, but I was not sure how the leadership of the church would react. During the worship that night, I could tell the pastor was upset. It seemed he was unhappy with the style of the music, how we dressed, and the gifts of the Spirit operating—even though people were saved and youth were excited about God and the event. The way the service flowed, it was evident that it went against the religious tradition of the church.

During this time in Belarus, we had a team of thirty who traveled with us from city to city doing outreach and production. Later that night after the event, when my outreach team and I were eating and resting from the night. I could hear the pastor scolding our tour manager about the service, even though everything was discussed beforehand. The pastor was still very unhappy. At that moment someone got up from the tour team and said, "I have a testimony! Philip, you know that word of knowledge you gave out during worship? Well, I had a tumor in the back of my left knee and it totally evaporated the minute you spoke out that word." Praise God!

As worship leaders, we must realize that when God speaks to us, we don't have time to disobey.

When the pastor heard that testimony, he realized that he was wrong and now had a new appreciation for the gifts of the Holy Spirit and that God can use this style of service to reach the lost. Because I obeyed God during worship, someone received their healing that day—and a pastor's outlook changed regarding how God can move. God is so good!

As worship leaders, we must realize that when God speaks to us, we don't have time to disobey. *Other people's blessings are on the other side of our obedience!* Whenever God says move, we have to move. Whatever God says to speak, we must speak. We can't delay. We can't wait for a more opportune time. We can't wait for the time that fits musically. We need to yield to do it in

His timing, not ours. We must be immediate in our obedience. When God says do it now, we have to do it now!

Sometimes those nudges from the Holy Spirit may be something as simple as a chord change during your set. It may not seem logical and even a bit unusual, but just trust Him. He knows what He's doing and where He wants to lead you and the people each time you gather to worship.

I remember playing during a particular meeting where an evangelist was praying for a woman who was oppressed by the devil. During this time of prayer and ministry, the Lord led me to just play this one chord. It didn't make sense to me, and I could have pridefully resisted His instructions. In fact, I didn't even like the chord—I liked what I was playing before! Everything in me said, "Don't do it!" But that still, small Voice inside whispered, "Follow Me." So, even though I had different plans and preferences, I followed that Voice.

Interestingly, the more I played that chord, the more it took on this war-like tone just as the evangelist was ministering deliverance to that woman. Together, we were all creating a corporate atmosphere for God to work in a marvelous way to deliver that lady from demonic strongholds. And praise God, she was set free by the power of Jesus!

I want to pause a moment here to share a technical nugget about holding a chord in worship. When we hold a minor deep chord (F#m / my favorite), it creates an atmosphere of war in the spirit. If that chord is played at the wrong time, it can produce a sad, depressing sound. However, if it's played in response to the leading of the Holy Spirit, it can reflect the depth of war that may be happening in the spirit, taking the worship into a completely different place.

In saying this I do not mean to say minor chords are evil. Chords and notes are created by our heavenly Father. We as believers can only produce what is inside us. If we put the Word of God and time spent with the Father inside us, that is exactly what we will produce. That is the anointing that will flow out of us. I am simply saying that chords placed strategically in a worship set can take us to a new level in the Spirit!

Conversely, when you hold a major chord, it will produce just the opposite effect. Instead of creating a fierce battle tone, a major chord will usher in worship. I suggest holding B♭ for a strong worship key. As God's saints rise in spontaneous worship and praise under that chord, you can feel the symphony of Heaven rising as well. This chord may even inspire a wave of prayer among the congregation!

Learning how a particular spiritual atmosphere can be created by using different chords is essential to your growth as a musician and worship leader.

Learning how a particular spiritual atmosphere can be created by using different chords is essential to your growth as a musician and worship leader. I encourage you to learn from other musicians as well. More importantly, you need to remember that the greatest teacher in the world lives inside you. Whenever you feel stuck or unsure what to do next, ask the Holy Spirit. He is faithful to teach you how to play the right chords at the right time, how to minister effectively through music, and how to flow with Him in every service.

In my personal experience, I've learned to rely on the Holy Spirit to teach me the dynamics of playing and the power of holding one particular chord. This technique has become a powerful weapon in my worship. It may sound a little boring and simple, but sometimes we have to learn to turn off our logic and just follow the Holy Spirit.

I do want to caution you not to become lazy and just automatically hold a particular chord because you're comfortable with it. If you do this, you and your band will come across as ill-prepared for the worship service. Be proficient and varied in your skill, but also make room for the Holy Spirit. When He leads you to play in a certain way, simply trust His instructions and follow Him. He knows what needs to happen in a service and what kind of atmosphere needs to be created through the musical sounds.

I hope you're now beginning to understand how important Spirit-led worship is to the ministry in God's house. As musicians, we play a critical part in creating an atmosphere for God to move in the way He wants to move in any given service. We can either open the door for God's Spirit to minister to others through our obedience, or we can close that door through our disobedience. God longs to demonstrate Himself, heal sick bodies, deliver people from addictions, and set people free from the bondages of darkness. But God is limited in how He can move if we refuse to follow Him. Learning to flow with the Holy Spirit and follow God's instructions are keys to leading transformational worship.

I want to encourage you—be ready to follow the Holy Spirit. Make it a point to listen to Him during worship. Keep your spiritual ears open and stay sensitive to His promptings. If He's leading you to go one way, don't be stubborn and go your way. Be humble! Be obedient! As you develop that ear to hear and that will to follow, you will be amazed how God's Spirit will minister to others in power and authority.

PRAYER

Father God, I thank You that the Holy Spirit is our teacher. That same anointing that raised Christ from the dead dwells in us. He teaches us. He anoints us. He leads us!

Today, I commit to listening to You as You lead me in worship. Even in the small details, I want to follow You. Whenever You lead me to change songs or play in a different key, I will do so. If You give me a word of knowledge, I'll speak it out. If You want us to sit in silence and listen to You, I won't say a word. I just want to obey You.

Lord, I give You free reign in our worship time. Teach us to follow You and flow with Your Spirit so that others may experience Your goodness. We don't want our plans, Lord. We want Your plans. May You be lifted up and Your name glorified!

In Jesus' name, amen.

CHAPTER 9

CULTIVATING A SPIRIT OF HUMILITY AND RELATIONSHIP

Perhaps the greatest challenge of all for worship leaders to overcome is the issue of pride. This one sin has been the downfall of countless staff members, choir directors, music members, and department leaders. It has been the root problem of hundreds of church splits and leadership rifts. And is it no wonder that satan himself was cast down from Heaven because of pride? The one who was celebrated for his musical gift in the heavens was also the one who was full of pride and vanity. Unfortunately, pride is still the number one downfall of worship leaders today.

To counteract this trap of pride, every worship leader and band member must have a revelation of humility from God's Word. I encourage you to take this subject very seriously in your personal devotion times. Find Scriptures about humility, write them down, and meditate on them. Commit them to memory.

Be obedient to them. Fill your heart with this truth. Look for examples in Scripture of humble people and how they walked in humility in the face of opposition. Hang around humble people in your church. Get to know God's character of humility. If you make it a priority in life to walk in Christlike character, you will be far less vulnerable to attacks from the enemy in the area of personal pride.

DISCERN THE SOURCE OF PRIDE

As a worship leader, this is an issue I've had to regularly overcome in my life. Far too often when I'm on the stage leading, the enemy will whisper in my ear, "You're doing so good. Look at all these people following you." Whenever I'm tempted with such thoughts, I have to stop and recognize who is behind them and why he is trying to pull me in that direction. If I give in to his thoughts and begin to develop an attitude of pride, I will become a stumbling block in God's Kingdom. It's so critical to discern the devil's tactics, resist him in the name of Jesus, and walk in freedom and humility. When I humble myself before God, Jesus is the One who is glorified!

People who do great things for God are at the core humble people.

One of the most important Scriptures to remember is James 4:10, *"Humble yourselves in the sight of the Lord, and He will lift you up."* People who do great things for God are at the core humble people. They don't have to brag about their gifts and talents, because they are patient for God to lift them up in due time. By waiting upon the Lord to open doors for them, they allow God to lead them and promote them. They are not trying to build their own kingdom—their greatest desire is to build up God's Kingdom.

Although you might be an awesome, qualified musician, I encourage you to wait for God to promote you. Don't talk about yourself and your talent and your ideas all the time. Let others acknowledge your gifts and let God do the lifting. This is one way in which you can cultivate a spirit of humility in your life.

LEARN TO RESPECT AUTHORITY

Sadly, many relationships in the Body of Christ have been wrecked because of pride. Relationships that were once beneficial and cooperative between pastors and worship leaders have been completely destroyed due to pride. It's a horrible device the enemy uses to stop the Kingdom of God from moving forward. Don't let that happen to you!

Although you might be an awesome, qualified musician, I encourage you to wait for God to promote you.

To maintain healthy, peaceful relationships around you, it's important to remain respectful of the leadership over you and over the house. For example, if you're ministering in a church service, you need to keep in mind that God has placed the pastor over that church as the senior leadership. That means if the pastor has laid down certain ground rules, you need to abide by them. Any attempt to overrule the pastor's authority—even when you think it is wrong and you are right—is an action of pride. Humble people yield their wills to those in authority.

The same principle applies to worship leaders on staff at a local church. You may have certain ideas or opinions on how the worship should be done; but if the pastor has an opposing opinion, you need to submit to that pastor. God put that pastor in charge of that local body. As a representative of God's authority in the Body of Christ, that pastor deserves your respect, not your disdain. So learn to bite your tongue, submit to authority, and maintain a good attitude even when you don't agree. This will help you immensely in resisting pride and cultivating humility!

Because I've had plenty of opportunities to practice humility in working with other pastors, I've learned some secrets that will help you overcome the temptation to override authority. For example, when I'm leading worship as a guest musician in someone's church, I ask the pastor how much time I have to sing or speak. If I'm told I can only have twenty-five minutes, then anything over that twenty-five-minute slot is of the devil because I openly disrespected the pastor's request. To take anything more than what has been given to me is disobedience and rebellion against authority. Because I want the blessing of God to remain on my ministry, I have to submit to God's authority in that house.

I ask the pastor how much time I have to sing or speak.

Respecting leadership is valid even when the pastor isn't Spirit-filled. As a Spirit-filled believer, I speak in tongues and flow in the gifts of the Spirit when I'm ministering. However, if I'm ministering at a church where the pastor does not permit those things to flow, out of respect for his or her authority, I will stay more neutral in my delivery and ministry while I'm in that church. I certainly don't want to cause strife or division, even when there's a slight difference in doctrinal beliefs. Because

I want to respect the rules of the house, I yield to the authority in that house. By implementing that simple courtesy of respect, not only have I nipped pride from blooming in my life, I've also maintained open doors of ministry with other denominations. That's a testimony of God's love and unity!

By honoring leadership and maintaining humility, we have the building blocks needed for true worship that brings in the presence of God. This is where worship *Rule 9: Be a servant to all, on stage and off stage,* can impact so many around you.

During the dedication of Solomon's temple in the Old Testament, the glory of God literally filled the house. Can you imagine what we have available to us today through the New Covenant? God longs to pour out His glory on those who worship Him!

May the enemy's weapon of pride be exposed, and may godly humility be a mark of your ministry.

My prayer for you is to encounter God's glorious presence every time you lead others into worship. In order for that to happen, you have to be a prepared, clean, and willing vessel. I pray that the truth of God's standards will become a mighty revelation in your heart and that you will exhibit Christlike character in word and deed. May the enemy's weapon of pride be exposed, and may godly humility be a mark of your ministry. God has called you in the Kingdom for this hour, and I pray you will rise up and lead people into the awesome presence of the King. May Jesus be glorified!

I truly believe that if you remain humble before God and submit to the authority God has placed in your life, you will become a catalyst for revival. True worship cannot happen without humility; and where there is no true worship, there is no true revival. Revival and true worship are two sides of the same coin. You simply can't have one without the other.

If the truth in this chapter has spoken to you, then take action. You might need to ask forgiveness from someone you disrespected. You might need to check the motives of your heart as to why you are serving where you are today. When you make a decision to humble yourself before God and people, God will push you forward into the destiny that He's prepared for you. Humility is the secret to both honor and revival.

John 4:24 instructs us to worship God *in spirit and in truth.* To worship Him in our spirit means to follow the Holy Spirit as He moves and flows through the different streams of praise and worship. Yielding to Him will cause you to humble yourself. To worship in truth means to worship in the revelation of truth from God's Word and to do the truthful and right thing. Submitting to authority and to the Word of God will also cause you to humble yourself.

Exchange your dreams for God's will for your life.

There's no easy road in God's way of doing things. However, if you are obedient to the Lord, He will move you forward in a way that we can't. I encourage you to take Jesus' yoke and burden, for the Bible says His yoke is easy and His burden is light (Matthew 11:30). Humankind's ways are tiresome and heavy, but God's ways are liberating and full of joy.

In finishing this point, I want to leave you with a critical mission—exchange your dreams for God's will for your life. Substitute your thoughts and plans for His thoughts and plans. This is the only way revival can come. Does it have a price? Yes.

It's the price of laying down selfish pride and picking up the cross of humility. This will cost you everything you have, but it will also bring the greatest rewards you could ever imagine. Humility is the price of honor and the doorway to revival.

THREE LEVELS OF HUMBLE RELATIONSHIP

> *Some will proudly claim, "I belong to the Lord." Others will say, "I am a descendant of Jacob." Some will write the Lord's name on their hands and will take the name of Israel as their own* (Isaiah 44:5 New Living Translation).

Honestly, I have read this verse many times, but got nothing out of it. Then the eyes of my understanding were opened, and I suddenly got it! I just love it when the Lord opens our eyes to see new revelation in the Word. What we have in this verse are three different levels of relationship we can have with God. Let's take this verse piece by piece, starting with Level One.

LEVEL ONE
"Some will proudly claim 'I belong to the Lord.'"

I can almost hear the sarcasm in the writer's voice in this part of the verse. I actually know people who talk like this. They say, "I'm a Christian" when it fits particular situations, like at Christmas dinner. They know when to nod their heads and say "Amen!" They know how to laugh at the Christian jokes; yet in their personal lives, they are far from knowing Jesus. They say what sounds religiously correct, but their lifestyles preach a different message. Jesus was savage the way He categorized these kinds of people. He called them "Hypocrites!" Jesus said,

> *What sorrow awaits you teachers of religious law and you Pharisees. Hypocrites! For you are like white-washed tombs—beautiful on the outside but filled on the inside with dead people's bones and all sorts of impurity* (Matthew 23:27 New Living Translation).

Ouch! It doesn't seem like Jesus was afraid of hurting people's feelings. No wonder the religious leaders wanted Him dead. The truth hurts and sometimes offends. Jesus was not afraid of being offensive. He cared more about speaking the truth, because the truth you know and experience will make you free. He wanted them to be free. Hypocrisy gives the Church a bad reputation. The world doesn't get it when you say you are a "Christian," but you live a double life. They have no problem saying, "You are a fake, and I want something that's real."

I remember witnessing to a guy who said, "I left the church because all of my friends are fake. I don't go to church because I want to sin and I won't hide it. But my Christian friends go to church to pick up girls, but they pretend to love God! That's messed up!"

God is real, and anyone who is truly living for God will have a lifestyle that proves it.

I totally agreed with the guy, but I was also able to open his eyes on the issue. I helped him realize that his friends' behavior was not real "Christianity." They had a form of godliness, but not real holiness. God is real, and anyone who is truly living for God will have a lifestyle that proves it. By the end of our conversation, I prophesied over his life and he was in tears. He said, "My dad has been praying for me for years. You are an answer to his prayers over my life. I needed this today, man."

My point is this: God doesn't like it when we live a double life. If you call yourself a Christian, then own it. Be like Cassie Bernall at Columbine High School who was shot to death for her faith. Because she professed her faith in God, she impacted hundreds of thousands of people worldwide. In the end, the gun was in her face and she said, "I'm a Christian." She owned up to who she was.

If you say you are a Christian but your life says otherwise, receive the truth, repent, and let it make you free. Fall on your knees and rededicate your life to God by saying, "God, I'm running *after* You, not *away* from You! I know Your arms are wide open. I'm asking You to forgive me. I no longer want to be the prodigal. I want to come home to You."

I can speak about this because I was that kind of Christian for a while. It takes one to know one! I thank God that I am not that kind of Christian any more. I chose to go to a higher level, and you can do the same. Don't wait till tomorrow. Do it now!

LEVEL TWO:
"Others will say, 'I am a descendant of Jacob.'"

I loved my grandpa. He was a godly man and he loved fishing. I can remember getting up at 4 a.m. to go with him to the lake. He always said that the best fish are caught before sunrise. Barely awake, I would get in the car and fall asleep while he drove. Sure enough, before five o'clock, we were pushing the boat into the lake. I loved it. We had a lot of fun, but I did it because he did it, and it was something that we were doing together. But he didn't take just me; he took all the grandkids.

While fishing with my grandpa, I often wondered if I would continue to enjoy it once he was gone, or if I was only doing it because I was with him. I knew that if I continued, then I was truly a fisherman. Well, that day came and I realized that I did it only because I wanted to be with him. Fishing was not my thing; it was just a "grandpa" thing.

This is a great example of a Level Two relationship. So many Christians live the faith of their parents, grandparents, aunts or uncles. But when those people are gone, so is their standard of living. Often, the loved one who is left behind backslides into the world, but that is not always the case. Some will stay faithful to the church if they have some level of a relationship with God. They will give their tithes but never really grab hold of the promises of God. They do it because their parents did it, not because they want to. They feel a sense of religious duty. They are faithful to show up out of obligation, not because they love the Lord. They won't rise to the next level with that mindset.

If it was typical of your parents to attend church only on Sundays, decide to go more often, attend a few services during the week. If they only read their Bibles while at church, decide to read yours every day. If they only prayed before going to bed at night, decide to rise early every morning to spend time with the Lord. If they never fasted and prayed, you decide to seek the Lord in a new and intimate way. If they immediately went to the doctor when they felt sick, you choose to plead the blood of Jesus and receive your healing today. If they were poor and lived with a poverty mentality, you begin meditating on the Word and God's promises to change your mentality to God's way of thinking. If they lived according to someone else's revelation, but that revelation never became a reality in their lives, you make it a reality!

Understand that, regardless of your parents' faith, you can live your own. Make a decision to know God for yourself and develop a personal relationship with Him. I made that decision. I remember the day when I was tempted to do something else with my life. But I decided to make my faith *mine,* and not just something my parents did. That day, my faith went from dormant to active.

I declare over you today that you are not sleepy—you are wide awake, vigilant, and ready to be used by God in a mighty way. Choose to go higher!

LEVEL THREE: "Some will write the Lord's name on their hands and will take the name of Israel as their own."

At Level One, we talk and act like Christians when it fits the situation. At Level Two, we're still underdeveloped in our faith and understanding, so we live off the faith, insight, and revelation of others. This is the stage at which we either stop growing in the Lord, or we get anxious and know that there has to be something more to this life than just being a churchgoer. We are eager to see a powerful move of God and need the answers. If this description sounds like you, then you are ready for Level Three, and God is ready to open your eyes to a new reality!

The third part of Isaiah 44:5 says, *"Some will write the Lord's name on their hands and will take the name of Israel as their own."* This is when your prayer life ceases to be just whispering words but actually becomes a vehicle of communication with your heavenly Father, fueled by the Spirit of God who will take you somewhere. This is when you go from preparation to action.

Often people will say, "I'm praying about what God wants me to do." You can run into those same people years later, and they are still praying about what God has probably already told them to do. They are stuck in preparation mode. Understand that I have nothing against a season of preparation; it's absolutely necessary! But a season of preparation doesn't last forever. At some point, that vehicle has to be fueled, turned on, and moved into action!

Imagine this. A warrior is training for battle. He tells himself every day, "I have to be prepared because the day is coming when I need to be ready to fight!" He listens to his instructors, studies, and stays alert, but when the battle begins, he says, "I need to stay home and prepare." That's foolishness! He would be considered unfit.

I know this sounds absurd, but this is often what Christians do. A battle is raging, yet we are just sitting at home preparing while the enemy is wreaking havoc. Start with what you have and what you know. Take the preparation you already have and act on it. Don't be the believer who prays about your calling for ten years while doing nothing. You are losing time. Start doing what you know to do today as you continue to prepare for whatever else God has for you in the future.

A great example of a person who progressed to Level Three is Gideon. When God found Gideon, he was working. It's been said that he was hiding while working in the winepress because he was afraid. Well, the location of the winepress was on enemy territory; thus, he was risking his life to provide for his family. That's pure courage! He wasn't just preparing to go into the winepress; he went in that winepress, prepared or not, to do what had to be done. It's no coincidence that God later found him in that same place and used him to save his nation from the enemy. He was faithful with little, so God gave him more.

God can still use us even when we are afraid as long as we're willing to move in faith. Our fear will turn into courage when we trust God. But we have to start doing something.

Our fear will turn into courage when we trust God.

Humble believers who are at Level Three know their dominion and authority in Christ. They also know that:

1. It's not about their name—it's about the name of Jesus.
2. It's not about their own authority—it's about the authority Jesus delegated to us by the Cross.
3. It's not about them—it's about God's plan and how it impacts others.

When God gives you an assignment, you must realize that it's not just yours. You are in Him. Acts 17:28 (NIV) says, *"For in Him we live and move and have our being...."* So you don't have to worry yourself sick about it or think, *Where will the money come from? What will people think when they see me? Where do I start?* Worrying about these things won't add a hair to your head. As a matter fact, you will probably lose hair and sleep in the process! God has all of those concerns settled, waiting for you to just show up and be ready. Just spend time with Him and take Jesus' name as your own. His name carries weight.

If you are called to be a worship leader, you won't always feel like singing or being 100 percent at every service. Some days, you will want to just stay in bed. You may even experience discouragement in your personal life while you're expected to uplift everyone else on the team and in the congregation. Remember that you are not in your assignment alone. God will strengthen and empower you if you just start singing with His goodness in mind. He won't leave you to struggle through every note. You are anointed, empowered, and equipped to do what you are called to do.

WHAT IS YOUR MOTIVE?

It's possible to do the right thing for the wrong reasons. When standing before God's people to lead them in worship, it wouldn't hurt to do a personal assessment and ask yourself the following questions: *Why do I do what I do at church? Am I doing it because it's my responsibility, or is it because I want to get on stage and glorify God? Am I focused on how I sound and how I look, or am I focused on Jesus?*

If you don't feel good about your answers, make the necessary adjustments, but never stop. View leading worship as a calling, not a job. It is a privilege, not a duty. This applies to anyone who holds a position of any kind in ministry. Do it because it's a privilege and honor to be appointed by God for such a task. Do it responsibly and unto the Lord. Everyone is blessed when you do.

View leading worship as a calling, not a job. It is a privilege, not a duty.

Ephesians 4:21 in the Passion Translation of the Bible says, *"If you have really experienced the Anointed One, and heard his truth, it will be seen in your life; for we know that the ultimate reality is embodied in Jesus!"* Here is the ultimate reality—Christ in you is the hope of glory (Colossians 1:27). And when you live your life with the right motives, the glory of God will be manifested in your life.

PRAYER

Father God, I lay down my ideas, dreams, and plans at Your feet. Help me discern the enemy's trap of pride so that I won't succumb to his temptations. I want only You to be exalted and glorified, Lord Jesus.

Create in me a clean, humble heart so that I reflect Your character to the world. Help me to respect the authority of others in Your house. I will work well with others and keep a good attitude even when I disagree with those You've put in charge. Help me to be an example of servant leadership to everyone around me.

With Your help, Lord God, I want to live in a Level Three relationship with You. May the Holy Spirit reveal ways to me so I can move from where I am in relationship with You right now to the next higher level, always striving to be closer and more Christlike with every breath.

Lord, I thank You for filling our services with Your glory. Thank You for changing hearts and transforming lives when we worship You.

In Jesus' name, amen.

CHAPTER 10

CONSECRATION AND DEMONSTRATION

Our worship is a reflection of our level of intimacy with God. It is a demonstration of how we know the Father on a personal level. Unfortunately, many worship leaders have become too focused on how they look, how they sound, and how people respond to them. When the crowd is pumped, they're pumped. They shine bright on stage, but when they're no longer in the spotlight, their light grows dim. They've reduced themselves to being performers instead of carriers of God's anointing. They have forgotten that it is the anointing that destroy yokes—not songs and music.

They've reduced themselves to being performers instead of carriers of God's anointing.

The power of music is divinely instituted. Music and sound can influence to affect every living thing exposed to the sound of it. Worship is uniquely inherent to the human experience. We all worship one thing or another. But we were created initially and ultimately to worship our heavenly Father, the Creator of Heaven and earth. However, it's hard to truly worship who you don't know. Just reading the Bible and saying routine prayers won't do it. We must spend quality time *with* God instead of just doing things *for* God.

We must spend quality time *with* God instead of just doing things *for* God.

We don't read our Bibles to gain points. We read to get to know our heavenly Father and to learn about His love, power, character, and concern for us. Praying isn't for the purpose of asking for everything we want—prayer is for the purpose of communicating with God about everything *He wants* to bring to pass on earth as it is in Heaven. And that, of course, includes His plan for our individual lives. That's how we learn His voice, understand His heart, and draw closer to Him. It's also how we become more like Him. God has always been devoted to us, but the depth and reality of our relationship with Him depends on our devotion and submission to Him.

It is fun seeing how my daughter is growing up, imitating my ways and becoming so much like me. The more time she spends with me, the more she talks like me, worships like me, and preaches like me. She knows me well because we're not just "related," we also have a close father-daughter "relationship." I may speak more firmly to her than I do to others at times, but I correct her when necessary because I love her and want to impart as much beneficial instruction as I can into her life. I want only good things for her. However, even though she is my daughter, it's totally up to her to decide if she will receive what I say with all her heart or disregard it. I'm grateful that her desire to be like her dad motivates her to take my words seriously. Her willingness to obey wise instruction makes her daddy proud.

Even though my daughter and I will always have a close relationship, its depth is determined by her willingness to receive my wisdom, knowledge, and love for her. As time goes on, our relationship will also be affected and influenced by my willingness to respect her right to choose how she will respond to my influence in her life. As her father, I will go after her wholeheartedly, but I can't force her to love and respect me. My hope is that she will always love me, if for no other reason than simply because she knows how much I love her.

The same is true in our relationship with our Father God. He revealed Himself to us when He sent Jesus, His Word to us wrapped in mortal flesh. Jesus told us in John 10:30 that He and the Father are one; and in John 14:9 Jesus says that when we see Him, we see the Father. Therefore, when Jesus laid His life down as a willing sacrifice on the Cross, He did so because the Father Himself wholeheartedly loved us before we could ever love Him (see John 16:27). We couldn't earn the Father's great love or forgiveness of sin because the substitutionary sacrifice of Jesus Christ, the Son of God, all took place while we were still sinners. Even now, we can never run too fast or too far without His love pursuing us. He has already given us all things that pertain to life and godliness (see 2 Peter 1:3), but He won't *make* us receive anything. He will never *force* us to love Him and to follow His commands. With lovingkindness He draws us to Himself. His desire is for us to respond to His unconditional love and concern—He does not desire to control us. God wants us to deepen our relationship with Him, but it will only go as deep as we allow it to be. We are the deciding factor.

If you are a true worshipper and love God with your whole heart, it will be evident first of all to Him, and then to everyone around you whether by your conversation, your actions, or by the way you respond to life's situations. You just can't hide it. It's impossible to be a true worshipper and your love for God not shine through. Jesus said that the one who really loves Him will keep and obey His commands (John 14:21). Therefore, when your love for Him is real, it will be obvious in your home, on your job, with your family members, and in your decisions. Your worship of God isn't just something you put on while you're on stage—your worship is how you live among people, and when people aren't even around.

It's impossible to be a true worshipper and your love for God not shine through.

There is a certain integrity and consistency about true worshippers—they are the same publicly and privately because they aren't living for the applause of the crowd; they live for the approval of God who always sees the heart. The thoughts and aspirations of the worshippers God seeks will soar high, like an eagle. As a result, they will lift people into the presence of God because His presence is where their own hearts call "home."

THE TWO WINGS OF WORSHIP

Not long ago, I started a study on eagles. I was fascinated not only by their physical attributes, but also by their development and practices. I discovered a few interesting parallels between their behavior and some character traits evident among those who press in to soar high in God.

First, and obviously, eagles have two wings that give them the ability to fly. If you want to destroy an eagle's life, all you have to do is cut off one of its wings. It will never fly again and do what it was designed by God to do. As worship leaders, we also have two wings that enable us to fly. One wing is a *personal consecration to God,* and the other is *public demonstration of that life.* If one of these wings is cut off, our ability to worship effectively fails. Our private, daily choices determine the strength of our "two wings of worship."

Let's take a look at some facts about the eagle. I think you will agree with me that eagles are amazing creatures.

- Golden Eagles have a wingspan that extends up to seven feet wide.
- A Golden Eagle can soar up to 15,000 feet in the air and glide effortlessly as it catches the air pockets at 65 mph.
- When in attack mode, an eagle can fly up to 200 mph.
- An eagle's eyesight is five times stronger than human eyesight.
- Excellent night vision enables the eagle to see with an ultraviolet light and detect the UV

reflecting urine from its prey.

- An eagle can even see with its eyes closed due to a translucent layer of skin on their eyelids called nictitating membrane.
- Eagles sleep while standing.
- An eagle will stand on one foot, while grabbing its prey with the other.
- Eagles continually clean their 25,000 different feathers to remove parasites and dust.
- Eagles realign their feathers to keep them in perfect condition so they can soar high.

Interestingly enough, the eagle imitates its parents from birth, doing everything it sees them do. It walks back and forth in the nest, which has borders that protects the young eagle from falling out. As the young eagle learns to flap its wings in order to fly, it starts by flying from branch to branch. But when it finally flies well enough to leave the nest, the eagle never returns to the nest of its birth. Flying forward, the young eagle establishes his own nest as his life journey begins.

We don't just worship on stage with our words; our worship spans the entire platform of our life.

What does the eagle have to do with a worshipper? Everything when you contrast an eagle's special features with the characteristics that are vital to a worshipper having a healthy walk with God. Consider:

- We don't just worship on stage with our words; our worship spans the entire platform of our life. No aspect of our life is to remain unmoved by Him. (See Psalm 147:1.)

- It glorifies Him when we know who we are, *Whose* we are, and we refuse to be blown away by opposing winds. Instead, we rise to catch the "wind pockets" of the Spirit—entering into the secret place of the Most High—and we mount up in Him, propelled in His presence to soar and even glide effortlessly, in Him. (See Isaiah 40:31.)
- Just as an eagle has exceptional night vision, we too can see when darkness surrounds us. His words are a lamp to our feet and a guide to our path. In His light we can see how to walk, how to discern with accuracy. We are to rely upon the eyes of our heart—spiritual eyes for supernatural vision—to help us distinguish what we can't detect. We must rely upon the light of God's Word to give us light when darkness seems to prevail. (See Psalm 119:105.)
- We stand firm in difficulties, trials, or adversity—even if on one leg, when we are tempted to be weak in our faith. And having done all to stand, we continue to resist the enemy and to triumph over him. (See Ephesians 6:13.)
- We keep ourselves clean and uncontaminated from the filth of the world by laying aside every weight, and the sin that would try to

attach to our lives so easily and undetected. (See Deuteronomy 23:9 and Isaiah 1:18.)

- We let the mind of Christ rule in us. Then, regardless of what may try to ruffle our feathers and get us off track, we continually realign ourselves with Him so we can keep making progress—fearing nothing and holding fast to His promises. (See First Corinthians 2:16.)
- We are imitators of our Father God, saying and doing what He says and does. And as we grow and mature in Him, walking in His identity being formed in us, we stop playing it safe within the boundaries of the familiar and the known. (See Ephesians 5:1-2.)
- Trained to walk by faith, in spirit and in truth, we leave our comfort zone, never returning to complacency. We focus our gaze on the Author and Finisher of our faith. And with the wind of God's Spirit beneath us, and the Word of the Lord within us, we rise to reach the purpose before us. We worship—and we soar as eagles. (See Second Corinthians 5:5-9.)

The majesty of an eagle in flight took on greater meaning and significance to me as I considered these parallels!

PRAYER, PRAISE, AND WORSHIP

I learn how soar above obstacles in the face of a great adversity. As a father, there is no greater trial than when your child is faced with a serious medical issue that seems hopeless.

I was praying with my youth worship team when I received a call from my wife. The phone call came about a minute before I was ready to go on stage to lead worship. Here's what she said, "Philip, the ambulance is here and they are saying that Mia (our daughter who was three at that time) is dying. She is coughing violently and can barely breathe. We are already on the way to the hospital."

In that moment I wanted to drop everything and run to my wife and daughter. As that thought came rushing into my mind, my wife immediately said, "Philip, you won't make it. It's rush hour, it's Moscow. All you can do is pray."

So you understand, the hospital my daughter was taken to in Moscow was seven miles away, even though this seems like a short distance by American standards, rush hour in Moscow by car would take an hour or more.

You can imagine what kind of effect this news could have on anyone getting ready to lead worship and I was no exception.

1. I felt like a terrible father because I couldn't be with my daughter and there to support my wife.
2. This kind of call really takes away all desire to worship with joy.
3. I had to lead others into worship when this burden felt like a heavy weight.

In that moment the words of my wife *shouted* in my head, "Philip, all you can do is pray." With tears in my eyes and an uncertainty of the situation, I told my wife, Ella, "God is with us. Everything will be okay!" As I hung up, I felt God's peace, but I was still fighting on the inside.

In that moment the words of my wife shouted in my head, *"Philip, all you can do is pray."*

As I went on stage, I told no one what was going on. At that moment, I remembered the Bible story of when the walls of Jericho fell because of praise! The Israelite king Jehoshaphat (2 Chronicles 20:20) sent the singers (Levite's) out into battle before the soldiers; and as a result, the enemy destroyed themselves.

In my heart I knew that if God did it for them, then He can do it for me. With all of this going on in my mind, I put a smile on my face, told the people God is good and began to lead the first song.

The first song was so hard. My mind was telling me, *Philip, be a good father and leave right now!* Another part of me was saying, *Put on smile and fight through it!* I heard God say, "Just praise Me."

I heard another voice tell me. "You are a hypocrite. You are putting a smile on. A mask! You are a big fat hypocrite putting on a smile when you don't feel like it." I realized this was not God's voice and honestly just ignored it.

When I would hear these thoughts go through my mind, I would fight and shout to the Lord all the more! I told the youth to worship, but it was dead. No one really reacted or praised. I was shouting, dancing, and praising all over the stage. I felt like I was the only one worshipping.

I got so into praise that by the third song, I forgot about my daughter! You might wonder how is that possible? How could I be so irresponsible? I was focusing on God and not the situation!

The only way Peter walked on the water was focusing on Jesus. As soon as he took his eyes off Jesus, he began to sink! My shouting, dancing, and praising was me looking at Jesus, my way of walking on the water!

It reminds me of the song that I love.

Turn your eyes upon Jesus, look
full in His wonderful face,

And the things of this earth will grow strangely
dim in the light of Your glory and grace!

I was walking on water! God gave me supernatural faith to soar! I was believing for a miracle and in perfect peace. I knew God was not worried so why should I? I finished worship, and thoughts for my daughter, Mia, flooded in.

I immediately called my wife and asked her how Mia was doing. Her reply, "Philip, the doctors do not know what happened! Out of nowhere she regained strength and started laughing, playing, and jumping!" The doctors were preparing for the worst, but God did a miracle!" My wife's prayer over our daughter and the sacrifice of praise on stage by faith caused our daughter to live. It truly was a miracle!

Praise is a powerful weapon. It saved my daughter. I was so thankful I didn't settle for the hand the devil dealt us. God has no favorites; we all have the same faith that resurrected Jesus from the dead living inside us according to Romans 8:11.

Like an eagle God taught me to soar over every obstacle. Like an eagle who is skillful in using the wind to fly through a storm to rise to new heights.

God doesn't want us to be consumed with anything or anyone but Him. Regardless of what's going on around us, pulling on us, or trying to distract us, we are to keep those things below us and to soar far above them by living in His strength. When we resist the downward pull of the cares of this life, we mount up high, having total faith in God's providence so we can freely worship Him for who He is.

The two wings of worship mentioned earlier—*a personal consecration to God* and *public demonstration of that life*—encompasses worship as a whole. Like the eagle, both wings must be intact. Let's take a closer look at what it looks like to have those two wings of worship actively engaged in our lives.

PERSONAL CONSECRATION TO GOD

What does it mean to walk in personal consecration to God? Personal means it is you and God—one on one, involving no one else. Consecration means your devotion to Him. In other words, when you are devoted to someone or to something, the person or object of your devotion is never far from your thoughts and you are always ready to interact with the object of your devotion.

When you are personally consecrated or devoted to God, it also means that you are completely transparent with Him, knowing that He sees your thoughts and the contents of your heart that are focused on and aware of Him. Personal consecration means that you esteem His thoughts and words above all others and above all else. Job 23:12 says, *"...I have treasured the words of His mouth more than my necessary food."* That is the heart declaration of someone who has a personal, practical, and thorough experience and knowledge of the Lord that isn't dictated to or derailed by anyone else.

Living a life of consecration means continually saying "Yes" to His will.

The worshipper who walks in personal consecration to the Lord receives God's encouragement and instructions as specifically and intentionally designed uniquely for him or her. If you've made the decision to live a life of consecration to the will of the Lord, that means you're not blowing off what He tells you to do just because others may not understand or agree. It means you remain committed to staying close to Him and putting Him and what He wants before everyone else. Living a life of consecration means continually saying "Yes" to His will.

We learn the heart and ways of God by spending time with Him, as already mentioned, and by reading the Bible. We wouldn't know anything about being born again if it wasn't written in the Word. That same Word teaches us what the sacrifice on the Cross is all about and what we're to know about God as our Father, Creator, Provider, Healer, and Peace. The written Word sets standards by which we are to live.

PUBLIC DEMONSTRATION OF A CONSECRATED LIFE

Our consecration to God is publicly demonstrated in many ways, starting with the level of faith we operate in daily. When you walk in the personal knowledge of God, you don't succumb to fear and anxiety. You don't fret or worry like a person who doesn't really know Him. Even when these negative emotions come on suddenly as an initial reaction to the unexpected, within minutes you will remember how groundless and unnecessary those reactions are.

The person who knows the Father and lives in continual communication with and consecration to Him, begins to recall God's faithful love and goodness in countless other situations and scenarios where fear tried to present itself as an option. Lovers of God know that He has their back and future—no matter what comes or goes. They know their times are in His hands. Fear can't conquer them because by the act of their own will in consecration to Him, God already has conquered their hearts!

When you are a true worshipper, walking in personal consecration, if you mess up (we all do), you will repent quickly, assured of His forgiveness. You will trust His every direction for your life because you rest in His faithful love.

Compassion is another public demonstration of our personal consecration to God. The word "compassion" is mentioned forty-one times in the King James Version of the Bible. Many Scriptures speak of how Jesus was moved with compassion and often changed His plans so He could meet people's spiritual and physical needs. His heart of compassion was cultivated through times of private consecration and communication with His heavenly Father. Your heart will swell with compassion in the same way because you take on the Father's character when you spend time with Him. It happens so naturally.

Compassion eliminates judgment, criticism, and ridicule of others. It makes room for humility on our part so that we see ourselves as a source of strength, encouragement, and peace for those who need it. Compassion for others helps us to put ourselves in others' shoes and, at least attempt, to feel what they feel and to see their situations from their vantage point. It's difficult if not impossible to worship God sincerely from an authentic place while we're in front of people if we're looking at different ones in the crowd with a judgmental attitude. That's pride and God will never be able to use you while you're operating in that attitude. He hates a haughty look and He will resist the proud. But when you humble your heart to allow His grace and compassion to flow through you, His goodness will manifest as you worship Him. And the lives of people you stand before will be changed.

Compassion eliminates judgment, criticism, and ridicule of others.

Sanctification is also the result of personal consecration. You can't help but live a sanctified life when you draw in close to God. You will rid yourself of everything that doesn't resemble Him or His love. As a matter of fact, the sight, sound, and sensation of sin becomes repulsive to you as your life becomes increasingly hidden in Christ. Your associations and sources of entertainment change. You no longer feel comfortable doing things that aren't pleasing to Him. You will also cringe at the thought of offending Him and others.

Appropriate *self-esteem or confidence* grows as a result of dwelling in the presence of God. When you learn about the privileges of your blood-bought covenant and understand your position at the right hand of God in Christ Jesus, you know that you can do all things through Him (Philippians 4:13). You don't shrink from receiving all that His sacrifice paid for and provides for you. You boldly expect every bit of it. With confidence, you ask for what you want and you receive what you need because you know Him as "Father," not just "God."

Some will equate your newfound sense of self-esteem with "arrogance," but don't let their assessment of you change anything. *Arrogance* comes into play only when you take credit for the good things that happen to and for you. "This happened because I...," and "This happened because I'm..." is arrogance. But, when you see yourself as valuable and capable because of *Him,* that's a true and pure sense of self-esteem. Others actually need to see this light in you because it's the only way to receive and enjoy every God-given benefit as His child. I learned and was reminded of worship *Rule 8: Must have a demonstration of your walk with God, on and off the stage.*

We must have a demonstration of your walk with God, on and off the stage.

People can be His beloved son or daughter and still live in defeat, disappointment, and despair if they don't know who they are. But I have confidence you are not going to that person, because you have God-esteem.

So it's important that your intimacy with Him builds your self-esteem so that others will want the same realization that it is

Christ, not their own works, who makes them worthy to become receivers of good things.

PRAYER

Father, I ask You to cultivate within me the heart of a true worshipper. Like the eagle, teach me to soar on the wings of Your Spirit. Teach me to understand the ebbs and flows of the Spirit.

Teach me to be disciplined in my walk with the Lord. I commit to You that I will not only be consecrated to You but there will also be a demonstration of that consecration through my daily life.

Because of my walk with the Lord, I have God's esteem and I am full of compassion for the world. Because of my consistent walk with the Lord, I will walk in authority and have a lifestyle of worship. Thank You for teaching and making me strong, in the name of Jesus I pray, amen.

CHAPTER 11

CLIPPED WINGS

Both wings are necessary for an eagle to soar high. But cutting off one of its wings isn't the only way to prevent that from happening; there is another way to destroy an eagle's life. It is more subtle, but potentially just as jeopardizing. All you have to do is *clip the tips* of both wings. Yes, the tips will eventually grow back, but when they are clipped repeatedly, the eagle never reaches its full potential because it thinks it can't fly. This is what happens to eagles in the zoo. Their wings must be clipped to keep them from trying to fly. Honestly, when I see such a beautiful bird caged as an exhibit, it's painful for me. But, it's a prime example of how great potential can be stifled.

I believe that the wings of many worship leaders have been clipped and are continually being clipped by their own choices and mindsets. The enemy clips their wings when they give in to his lies suggesting that the most important things in worship are the quality of the songs, the expertise of the leader and musicians, the teamwork, how well the music entertains, and the marketing potential. Don't get me wrong; these things are important. But if we make them the primary focus, we miss the whole point of why we worship. The purpose of singing worship songs isn't to try to become famous; the purpose of worship is to make *Jesus* famous.

The purpose of singing worship songs isn't to try to become famous; the purpose of worship is to make Jesus famous.

I have a lot of respect for anyone who sings in stadiums before thousands worldwide. It's awesome to see what God can do through people. But I have just as much respect for someone who has a consistent prayer life behind closed doors. The person praying behind closed doors is actually fueling what's taking place in the stadiums! It's very possible that no one will ever see that person in prayer. Yet, his or her assignment is extremely vital for the Kingdom of God. In fact, it's huge in God's eyes.

When you are willing to devote your time to seeking God and His will in private, God can trust you with His wisdom and power publicly because you've proven that your priorities are in agreement with His. You can be both a worshipper and an intercessor. In fact, you *should* stand before God on behalf of people before you attempt to stand before people on behalf of God.

Here is another lie that clips our wings—your worth as a worship leader is determined by the number of people you lead in worship. I've caved in to that lie while comparing myself to others. Those who compare themselves among themselves are not wise (2 Corinthians 10:12). That's especially a challenge when it comes to social media. I would go through my news feed and "like" everyone who was doing something for the Lord while I felt like I wasn't doing much at all.

Sometimes we need to turn off our phones and computers and realize that our identity is not in what we do—it's in what God says about us. There is nothing in the Bible that says God's love and approval of us is based on how many follow us and "like" us. God is simply looking for those who are passionate about worshipping Him with their whole heart. *"God is Spirit, and those who worship Him must worship in spirit and truth"* (John 4:24). Those are the ones the Father will seek after.

If you are obedient to the Lord's call to sit in a room and pray alone, you are just as significant and beneficial to the Kingdom of God as someone who is obedient to the Lord's call to speak before thousands in stadiums. Obedience is what makes you valuable to the Lord and it is your willing obedience that determines your reward from Him.

It's so unfortunate to see people compare themselves to others and begin to lose their own footing until they start to slip and possibly derail off track. I can honestly say that the reason I did not completely backslide as a young man is because my mom and dad were praying for me. You might say, "Philip you're a missionary's kid, a pastor's son. How could that happen?" Satan doesn't discriminate. His tactics are the same for everyone, regardless of who or what they are.

But the way God got me out of the enemy's grasp was through their fervent prayers. *The prayer of a righteous person is powerful and effective"* (James 5:16 NIV). The way He will get you out is through prayer. The way He will get your family out is through prayer. Prayer is powerful. Fervent, heartfelt prayer and worship release the will of God into situations, causing the invisible to become visible and the intangible to become tangible.

You may never travel; you continue to lead worship from the same pulpit at your church Sunday after Sunday. Well, let me encourage you. Guest ministers will leave your city and go to the next city, but someone has to stay behind and continue to fuel the fire, fan the flames, and keep the worship team motivated. It's work, and sometimes it might seem hard and boring, but it's work that produces results for the Kingdom of God in that house of God. The key to effective productivity is to keep the worship of God rising strong in your own private time. Proclaim the awesomeness of God and glorify Him for everything when no one is around. Encourage your worship team to do the same, reminding them that worship must come from the heart. Whatever takes place in private will fuel and influence what happens in public.

Never be lured out of your lane with a lie sprouting from a root of insecurity.

Whether you pray unseen in a room, lead worship in church before the same people each Sunday, or travel the world to sing and preach the gospel, you are doing it all for the glory of God. Therefore, you *are ne*cessary! Never be lured out of your lane with a lie sprouting from a root of insecurity.

GOD WANTS YOU TO SHINE

Believers in Jesus Christ have a great opportunity to shine brightly in a dark world. Jesus said we are the salt of the earth, the light of the world, a city set on a hill (Matthew 5:14). We shouldn't try to hide it. Our light is to be seen in the power and the authority that we carry. I'm not just talking about on Sundays; I'm talking about every day we live.

It's a great honor to stand on stage and lead God's people in worship. I can't think of any honor that could even remotely surpass it. As worship leaders or musicians, we are singing and playing for the King of kings and Lord of lords. What could possibly be more exciting than that!

I know that some have expressed the view that worship music is too simple and they want to venture into something different or to develop themselves in another type of music. I've seen people leave worship teams for this very reason. They've been conned into believing a lie. The enemy wanted to clip their wings. Although there's nothing wrong with playing and singing other styles of music, nothing beats being used as a mouthpiece for God. And He is a very creative God! The magnificence of His creation is evident everywhere we look.

For example, I'm fascinated with hummingbirds. I'm awed at every intricate detail in their colorful feathers. I enjoy watching their wings moving at what appears to be the speed of light. Every aspect of a hummingbird reflects God's beautiful artistry as the Creator. Also, when I look into the eyes of my wife and children, I see our Creator's touch—so much beauty and so much detail. I think to myself, *God, You truly create beautiful things. Your creative abilities are limitless.* And, guess what? That same creative power is resident within you and me.

We have access to an unlimited reservoir of creativity and inspiration because of the Spirit of God. We never have to settle for being copies of someone else or of reproducing something someone else has made. I encourage all worship teams to be open to new ideas instead of imitating what others are already doing. Ask God to unlock and release your creative abilities, then allow the Holy Spirit to lead and guide you into your own uniqueness and creative space. God is faithful. He will show you how to invigorate the worship music you already use.

God knows how to add just the right amount of flair to every song. He is not a God of boredom. Most of all, once He anoints a song, a singer, or a musician, life and power will be the most notable qualities about them, and the divine touch will be evident to all. Seek the Lord; surrender yourself and your purpose to Him as you invite Him to invade and to direct all you're doing. When you do, then watch your songs go from simple to beautiful, impactful, and supernatural. God's design and desires for what we're doing far outweighs our own. Therefore, we shouldn't limit ourselves to our ideas when we can tap into divine inspiration and creativity—continually!

Creativity can be used in every walk of life whether you're in business, the arts, media, sports, or even parenting.

Creativity can be used in every walk of life whether you're in business, the arts, media, sports, or even parenting. Just as we are uniquely created, so are our skills. We may not have been aware of them, especially if we're used to doing the same old thing over and over again and have never gone out on a limb and tried something new. Nevertheless, the unique skills are there. God doesn't want you to produce something that is ordinary. *God wants you to produce something that's extraordinary as a trademark of His greatness in you.* He wants to drop something right out of Heaven that will truly leave you and others speechless. Aren't you ready for God to blow you away by His own greatness? All you have to do is follow His voice and walk out the path He sets before you.

WORSHIP VERSUS ENTERTAINMENT

The world's music may have a great beat and great lyrics that make you want to move. But it's no comparison to the music that comes from Heaven. Our focus is not to capture a style that moves people. We want to release a sound that moves Heaven to earth!

Styles of music reflect preferences. But spiritual substance in music is a direct result of the anointing of God. The style of music I enjoy singing a lot is jazz. In fact, years ago, I was called and asked to sing for several events. I did it for a little bit, but it just didn't feel right. I resisted God's promptings on the issue because I enjoyed the style of jazz. But of course, God won and I no longer accept invitations to sing jazz.

I learned the difference between merely using my talent versus living in my call.

Though I really enjoyed singing other music, I noticed that it was pure entertainment. As I sang those big band hits, people clapped and cheered. But I felt like I was covered in dirt. In fact, it felt like I was doing something second best—like eating cheap noodles instead of a steak dinner. Everything about it felt wrong because I was built for so much more. I learned the difference between merely using my talent versus living in my call. I also learned the importance of following my purpose—which is timeless—instead of giving into my passion—which is temporary. My purpose became my passion!

The Lord taught me the difference between entertainment and worship. When I sang for the world—even morally good songs—I was merely entertaining everyone's flesh and soul, while leaving their spirits empty. But when I stand on stage and sing worship songs, I'm stirring up everyone's spirit, drawing their hearts and minds into a place of worship to glorify God. I'm impacting eternity!

When I quit the world's music and started singing only what Heaven sings, Matthew 16:19 came alive to me: *"...whatever you bind on earth will be bound in heaven, and whatever you loose on earth will be loosed in heaven."* That's powerful. When you let loose in worship here on earth, the heavens let loose. Chains fall off, people receive their healing, and souls come under conviction. The angels of God recognize His voice coming through the words of your worship songs. When you do Kingdom business on earth, Kingdom business is happening in Heaven that will impact eternity.

When music involves the heart of God, it can change the hearts and lives of people.

Maybe you are reading this and thinking, *I'm not a worship leader, I'm in Christian mainstream music—so what does this have to do with me?* I respect Christian mainstream when the words and music are written with a Christian perspective. However, our motive and focus must be radically different from the world. I don't believe we have to be like the world in order to reach the world. I believe that if we follow God's heart and plan, we will draw people to Him. When music involves the heart of God, it can change the hearts and lives of people. Proverbs 11:30 (NIV) says, *"...the one who is wise saves lives."*

In my case, I was singing songs that weren't Christian and were written from a soulish place instead of the Spirit. Music originating from the Spirit flowing through our spirits will lift people out of their souls into a spirit-to-Spirit encounter with the Lord, where He can cause their thoughts to become agreeable with His will. Music that pours out of our souls, however, will only stir the souls—emotions and thoughts—of others, leaving them stuck and focused on their own thoughts and feelings instead of on the One who can lift them up and out and change everything.

That's why singing jazz didn't feel right for me. I was singing from a soulish place based on my own preference and enjoyment of that music. Although others enjoyed it and wanted me to continue, they were never moved in their spirits to draw near to God. They were just soothed, stirred, or entertained emotionally, which kept them self-focused instead of God-focused. No wonder the Lord was not pleased. I was using the gift He gave me to help people remain self-indulgent instead of using the vehicle of music to access the presence of God. I now encourage all Christian musicians to write evangelistic songs that are written from the heart of God to lift the thoughts and focus of people off themselves or their circumstances—good or bad—and to bring their perspective in sync with the One who has a plan for them and their future.

"Can worship music still entertain the flesh and soul?" This question was raised while talking with my friend and worship assistant, Timothy Grahame-Smith , about the difference between entertaining the soul and impacting eternity. His answer was "Yes." I was shocked! The truth of the matter is that when people on stage don't have a relationship with God, they are merely doing a job. They will impact the soul, but won't stir up people'

spirits or impact Heaven. All eyes will be on the ones who are singing instead of lifted up to God.

We've all witnessed instances when one person would sing a song, and we said that it was good. But then someone else sang that same song, and the power of God showed up and His anointing filled the place. The same song was sung by two different people in two different places, but one sang it from pure talent, musical knowledge, and from the soul. And the other sang it from a place of reverence, overwhelming love for God, and from the heart while using their talent. Both reflected what was inside—one, his fleshly desire to entertain, and the other, a passionate desire to worship to God. The latter more than likely spent sweet quality time with God privately at home before going on stage.

THE POWER OF THE SECRET PLACE

Your greatest moments with God don't start on stage; they start in the secret place with Him. Jesus was constantly going to the secret place. Mark 1:35 (NIV) says, *"Very early in the morning, while it was still dark, Jesus got up, left the house and went off to a solitary place, where he prayed."* Why did Jesus do this? He didn't want to operate from His flesh; He wanted to operate in the supernatural from the Spirit.

You might say, "Wait a minute, Philip. How could Jesus operate from a place of the flesh? Wasn't He God?" Absolutely! But He chose to lay aside the rights and privileges of operating as God so He could fully engage the human experience, to be touched with the feeling of our weaknesses as a Man, living in a human body like ours. And, just like us, He had to constantly spend time with the Father to rise above and endure temptation.

> *Who, being in very nature God, did not consider equality with God something to be used to his own advantage; rather, he made himself nothing by taking the very nature of a servant, being made in human likeness. And being found in appearance as a man, he humbled himself by becoming obedient to death—even death on a cross!* (Philippians 2:6-8 NIV)

Jesus had to *choose* to live out of His fellowship with the Father in every area of His natural life while here on earth. He said what He heard from the Father, and He did what the Father revealed to Him in prayer. While on earth, He was *"Jesus of Nazareth,"* but *"God was with Him"* (Acts 10:38). We must allow our deep, intimate communion with the Father to control our decisions and to direct us into living by the Spirit, refusing our flesh to exercise its carnal influence. The Bible says that in every way we're tempted, Jesus was tempted. But with every temptation, there is a way of escape. Jesus showed us that private time with the Father in prayer is key to avoiding temptation.

Spending private time with His Father kept Jesus focused and on track so He could say, *"the Father who dwells in Me does the works"* (John 14:10), and John 8:29: *"I always do those things that please Him."* Keeping a constant connection with the Father kept Jesus on target. That connection will do the same thing for us. We see in the Gospels that after ministering to the crowds, Jesus often pulled away from people to go to secret places to be alone with God. It was a necessity to maintain a pure and vital connection with the Father so Jesus could say, *"Anyone who has seen me has seen the Father"* (John 14:9 NIV). The same is true and necessary for us as well. When doing this, we are applying worship *Rule 10: Your power and success come from intimacy and time alone with God.*

> *He who dwells in the* ***secret place*** *of the Most High shall abide under the shadow of the Almighty* (Psalm 91:1).

Living in complete surrender to God keeps our spirit strong and keeps our flesh in check at all times.

Living in complete surrender to God keeps our spirit strong and keeps our flesh in check at all times. Fleshly ideas don't have longevity because there's no real life in them. Ideas that are born of the Spirit will release supernatural activity that destroys the plans of the enemy. Keep in mind that God never has to come up with anything. He already has every answer waiting for our questions, problems, needs, and wants. He is never at a loss for new and exciting ways of doing anything. He is God!

TESTIMONY OF WHAT PRAYER IN THE SECRET PLACE CAN DO

One cold Ukrainian winter in the city of Perevalsk, a teenager was returning home from a club. She could barely walk because of the amount of alcohol she had consumed. She eventually made it to her grandmother's house where she was living at the time. Her grandmother was a prayer warrior who stood in the gap for her 24/7.

When the teenager was six, she talked to the Lord all the time. She talked to Him and sang songs to Him daily as she walked through the snow to and from school. She loved Jesus; but after her parents were divorced, her heart grew cold toward God and she lost the intimacy with Him she once had. Her grandmother, however, continued to believe in her granddaughter's calling and knew that she would one day return to her First Love. So the grandmother spent hours every day reading the Word and praying for her granddaughter.

The house was permeated with the presence of God, so it was no surprise that when the teenager returned home drunk that night, she heard a Voice as she collapsed on her bed. Almost asleep she heard, "Before you is life and death, choose life" (Deuteronomy 30:19). When she heard the Voice, she immediately became sober. She knew exactly who was speaking to her. She also knew it meant that a serious life change was imminent.

In submission to her grandmother, the girl moved from Ukraine to Moscow to attend school and started attending church. She rededicated her life to the Lord, and God began doing a work in her. She later began dating a boy in the praise and worship team, who happened to be the pastor's son. After a few more years, they were married.

That girl from Ukraine is my wife, Ella Renner, and this is her testimony! That day in Perevalsk, she chose how deep she wanted her relationship with God to go. She had to choose life or death. She chose life.

God is asking you the same question. What will you do? Will your relationship with Him be surface level for your whole life, or will you allow God to dig deep into your soul and change your relationship with Him—improving every aspect of your life? If you choose life like my wife did, your life will change for the better in ways you can't now imagine.

PRAYER

Heavenly Father, the Creator of Heaven and earth, to be consecrated before You, we know we must spend quality time with You instead of just doing things for You. We must read our Bibles to learn about Your love, power, character, and concern for us. Praying to You will reveal Your plan for our individual lives. Praying is how we learn to hear Your voice, understand Your heart, and draw closer to You.

Lord God, You have always been devoted to me, but the depth and reality of my relationship with You depends on my devotion and submission to You. I pledge to seek You, Lord; I surrender myself and my purpose to You and ask that You direct all my ways.

Beginning right now, I will allow my deep, intimate communion with my heavenly Father to control my decisions and direct me into living by the Spirit, refusing my flesh to exercise its carnal influence. Jesus has shown me that private time with the Father in prayer is key to avoiding temptation. Spending private time with His Father kept Jesus focused and on track so He could say, "the Father who dwells in Me does the works" (John 14:10). I want to be able to say the same.

In Jesus' name, amen.

CHAPTER 12

TAKING ACTION

I am so thankful that you have taken the time to read this book. I pray that it has expanded your knowledge of the principles governing true, biblical worship. My prayer is that the message conveyed in this book will help you grow both spiritually and practically.

Applying knowledge is the definition of wisdom.

Moreover, I pray that you take the knowledge you have attained and apply it to life. Applying knowledge is the definition of wisdom. Just reading the book without application will not do much; but if you apply the insight in this book, it will help you reach your potential as a believer, worshipper, and leader. These truths will cause your team to grow and will help you to understand your pastor better. Most of all, doing what is in this book will generate greater unity with your team, your pastor, and your church—discovering that miracles are not only possible, they're inevitable!

One of my favorite Scriptures revealing the power of unity is found in Genesis 11:6 (KJV):

> *And the Lord said, Behold, the people is one, and they have all one language; and this they begin to do: and now nothing will be restrained from them, which they have imagined to do.*

In context of this passage, the people were all focused on one thing—building the Tower of Babel. Their unity alone could have empowered them to accomplish their singular vision. Whatever they imagined, they had the power to do just because they were so bound together in united focus and effort. Unity is an amazing force that can generate powerful results, if we learn to work together toward *God's* plans and purposes.

Communication is essential in building unity, and when the lines of communication are clogged, it can bring confusion and hinder teamwork.

On a final note, I'd like to encourage you to keep the lines of communication open between you, your team, and your pastor. Communication is essential in building unity, and when the lines of communication are clogged, it can bring confusion and hinder teamwork. It's important for you as a leader to be constantly in contact with your team. Call, send text messages, email updates, or videos to encourage them and get the job done. Connecting with your team is easy, especially with the many different media avenues available now. You'll be amazed how a simple text can build comradery and boost morale with your team.

If communication isn't your strong point, you can still build unity by being mindful of your team and the hard work they're doing. Instead of taking your team members for granted, learn to communicate respect and appreciation to them in both verbal and nonverbal ways. A thank you goes a long way in showing honor to your team and makes those you lead feel valued and special.

For example, after a practice session or a service, you can send a text to your band that says something like this: *"Today was powerful! Thank you for all of your hard work. Because of everyone's deposit, the Lord's plan was fulfilled."* A message like that literally takes less than two minutes of your time, but the impact it can have on your team is priceless. Your communication doesn't have to be long or complicated—just be sincere and encouraging in your words and actions toward those you lead.

One word of caution—be careful not to send only instructional content to your team. Although task-oriented messages are important, you need to be encouraging as well. Remember, the people you work with are not just musicians, they're also people with real needs and feelings. If you never write or call to say thank you, your team will think you're a taskmaster. That kind of leadership and organizational culture is not the best environment for team building and unity.

While communication is a natural tool, poor communication can delay what God wants to do in the spiritual realm. Remember, it takes both the natural and the spiritual working together to produce transformational worship. Prayer is powerful and practicing is powerful, but if you don't have strong communication, revival through worship will be put on hold. Assumption is the lowest level of communication, so don't just assume things are done. Double check with your team and delegate tasks.

If you want to be a great leader, start by pouring your life into other members of your team.

Here's the good news. You don't have to lead all by yourself! In fact, leading by yourself is pointless. If you want to be a great leader, start by pouring your life into other members of your team. Build disciples as Jesus did. Have coffee with team members, invite them to your home, pray with them, and have fun. Jesus did this with His disciples, and they in turn took the Gospel to the ends of the earth.

TAKEAWAY KEYS

To help you review and remember some of the important principles we covered in this book, I've compiled the following section as a quick reference guide for Chapters 2 through 11. These takeaway keys can be used as an easy resource when you need to refer to a valuable nugget or Scripture verse. I encourage you to highlight these points, study the Scriptures, and share them with your team.

CHAPTER 2 TAKEAWAY KEY: Prepare Yourself

If you're a worship pastor, leader, or team member, preparation is essential. You must constantly prepare yourself spiritually and professionally. It's also important to keep in mind that as gifted and talented as you are, you are also replaceable. Lack of character, responsibility, and teamwork can close the doors God had opened for you. This is something I remind myself of every day!

You must constantly prepare yourself spiritually and professionally.

The moment you stop preparing yourself is the moment someone else could take your call. I know this may sound harsh, but it's true! No one wants to work with someone who is lazy or difficult to work with.

The reality of unfaithful stewardship can be seen in the parable of the talents (see Matthew 25:14-30). The lazy servant who didn't do anything with his talent was reprimanded by the master for his deliberate unfaithfulness. Consequently, his talent was actually taken away from him and given to someone else. Can you imagine how disappointed the lazy servant must have been with the reality his laziness created? Ouch! I encourage you not to be like that guy!

The time you have on this earth to do what God's called you to do is short. You don't have the luxury to procrastinate! You must be busy working on the Father's business.

Also, it's important to remember that whatever you pour into yourself is what will eventually come out of you. Because you're like a sponge, you need to regularly soak up the Word and prepare yourself professionally. If you are faithful to saturate yourself in God's Word, then when the time comes for God to squeeze you, the Body of Christ will be blessed wherever you go.

Study Scriptures

- Matthew 25:14-30
- Luke 19:12-27
- Luke 16:10
- Proverbs 28:20
- Proverbs 12:24

CHAPTER 3 TAKEAWAY KEY:
Build on God's Word

As you're leading worship, remember the Word of God is the foundation of worship. Jesus tells us that true worshippers will worship Him in spirit and in truth. The truth is the Word of God.

One way to keep worship grounded in God's Word is to start off the worship time with a Scripture and then continue weaving Scriptures in between songs. This practice will help generate unity among the people and bring their focus on the Word.

Also, it's important to select songs that are built on God's Word. There are a lot of songs out there that reflect emotion instead of truth, or doubt instead of faith, but these songs don't do anything to help people grow up in God. When choosing your set, make sure the songs you pick are doctrinally correct and come from the Bible. Remember that music doesn't have the power to change people's lives—only God's Word and His Spirit can do that. So be careful to put God's Word first in worship and build your music upon that solid foundation of truth.

Study Scriptures

- John 4:24

- Hebrews 4:12
- Matthew 4:4
- Acts 4:31
- 2 Corinthians 6:7

CHAPTER 4 TAKEAWAY KEY: Lead the People

As a leader, you bear the responsibility of leading people in the right way. Remember, those gathered are looking to you and your team during worship for direction and instruction. You can't expect them to do what you're not showing and instructing them to do. Set the tone and be the example for them to follow in worship.

At the start of service, politely ask the people to greet each other. During appropriate times in worship, quote God's Word to them, have them quote the Word to each other, suggest to them to raise their hands, shout unto God, or fall on their knees. As you stay sensitive to the leading of God's Spirit in the flow of worship, you are responsible to lead others into that flow.

If you're struggling with giving direction and instruction to the congregation, just remember that you are a worship leader submitted to God and to the pastoral authority in that house. There are plenty of Scriptures supporting your responsibility to lead others into worship.

Whenever you feel overwhelmed with how to lead or what to say, start by encouraging the people with stories from your own life. Share from your heart and testify of God's goodness in your own life. You'll soon discover that a sincere approach will always encourage people in opening their hearts to worship.

Study Scriptures

- Psalm 23:6
- Psalm 27:13
- Psalm 31:19
- Psalm 29:2
- Psalm 95:6

CHAPTER 5 TAKEAWAY KEY: Communicate Verbally and Nonverbally with Your Team

Communicating with your team members is essential in leading a worship service. In fact, I can't stress enough the importance of correct body language with your team on stage. As an example to the church, you and your music team need to look like a family. That means you move together, smile together, shout together, lift the name of Jesus together, and intimately have a good time together during worship. When people see positive family dynamics on the stage, chances are they will want to be part of the church family!

Study Scriptures

- Galatians 6:10
- Ephesians 3:15
- Matthew 18:15
- Mark 11:25
- Romans 14:17

CHAPTER 6 TAKEAWAY KEY: Choose the Right Key and Melody

When selecting keys and melodies for your worship music, it's critical to choose something that works for the majority. If people can't sing a song because it's too high or too low, there will be no unity. And when there's no unity, it's not worship—it's just a concert!

The same principle applies to the melody. If people can't sing a particular tune because the melody is too complex, then this song will not work for congregational worship. Again, a complicated melody doesn't produce unity among the people.

A simple rule of thumb to follow is if the congregation can't learn a new song in five minutes and sing it comfortably, then the song isn't a good fit for congregational worship. I know this is a basic concept, but it has spiritual applications. When songs are too complicated, there will be no unity—and it's unity that sets the environment for miracles.

Study Scriptures

- 1 Chronicles 15:16
- 2 Chronicles 5:13
- 2 Chronicles 7:6
- Ephesians 4:3
- Psalm 133:1

CHAPTER 7 TAKEAWAY KEY:
Maintain Necessary Eye Contact

Your eyes are truly the windows into your soul, and proper eye contact communicates volumes to others. People can tell if you're being fake, insincere, or inattentive when they look at your eyes. On the flip side, your eyes can also convey warmth, care, understanding, and compassion. You can even preach the light of the Gospel with your eyes!

Because eye contact is imperative to communication, you need to be mindful of when and where you're looking during worship. Remember to keep your eyes open at all times when you're leading from the stage. People online lose connection when your eyes are closed, and the people in the audience want to see your beautiful eyes. By keeping your eyes open, you maintain proper eye contact with the people, your team, and the pastor. Ultimately, as connection is being communicated through your eyes, you are helping to establish unity within the congregation. And an environment of unity sets the atmosphere for miracles!

Study Scriptures

- Genesis 6:8
- Proverbs 15:30
- Proverbs 23:26
- Psalm 19:8
- Psalm 34:15

CHAPTER 8 TAKEAWAY KEY: Follow the Holy Spirit

In everything you do, remember to follow the leading of the Holy Spirit. God is always endeavoring to speak to you and lead you, but the choice to follow Him is up to you. You can either follow your own plan or you can follow God's plan.

I believe in following the schedule of a service, but if the Holy Spirit wants to switch things up and the pastor is on board with it, then follow His leading. Don't be held hostage to the schedule, because King Jesus is Lord over the schedule!

If you feel the Holy Spirit wants to move in the gifts of the Spirit—such as prophecy or word of knowledge—go ahead and yield to Him. We can't predict times when the Holy Spirit wants to move like this, so it's impossible to "schedule" spontaneous time of ministry. Whenever the Holy Spirit does lead you to move in the gifts, simply surrender the schedule to Him and obey.

When I sense a flow of the gifts of the Spirit, I'm often concerned that I will go over the allotted time if I follow His leading. However, I've discovered that usually the gifts of the Spirit happen during appropriate times within the service, bringing order instead of chaos. In the end, all are blessed.

I encourage you to be jealous for the things of the Spirit. Pray in tongues, and lead the people in the flow of the supernatural. When you're yielded to the leading of the Holy Spirit, you help create an atmosphere of unity and miracles!

Study Scriptures

- 1 Corinthians 12:4-11

- 1 Samuel 10:6
- Acts 2:17-18
- Romans 12:6
- 1 Thessalonians 5:20

CHAPTER 9 TAKEAWAY KEY:
Submit to Authority

In His wisdom, God set up His house with certain leadership and governance. He established the pastor as the primary overseer of the local church, and it is his or her responsibility to lead and guide the flock.

When you recognize that your place as a worship leader or band member flows underneath the authority of the pastor, your supply to the Body will be much more powerful. God can do what He wants to do in a service when you are submitted to authority and operating in unity and harmony.

It's important to keep in mind the authority God established in His house. The Holy Spirit will never tell you to go against the authority of the pastor. In fact, being in submission to the pastor is a big part of being led by the Spirit, because you are submitting to God's order set forth in His Word.

Sadly, many churches have experienced great division because people were not submitted to the pastor's leadership. God doesn't go against the order He established. However, when people rebel against God's ordained authority, it will bring great harm and division to a local congregation.

If you as a worship leader will submit to those whom God has put over you, God will lift you up in the future. The Bible says God resists the proud but gives grace to the humble. One of the greatest lessons you can learn is humility. It's the key to any future promotion!

Study Scriptures

- 1 Corinthians 12:18
- 1 Corinthians 12:23-31
- Ephesians 4:16
- 1 Peter 4:10
- 1 Peter 5:5-6

CHAPTER 10 TAKEAWAY KEY: Consecration and Demonstration

The only way you and I will be truly successful in worship is if we have a strong relationship with God. God has given us all the power and authority we need through His sacrifice on the Cross.

Like the eagle, we can soar over every obstacle; and as the eagle catches the air pockets, we catch those spiritual air pockets, winds, that will propel us into our future. There is only one thing we must do: fall in love with Jesus with all our heart. Consecrate, commit ourselves to Him but don't stop there! Demonstrate that power through our daily life. If we do not demonstrate His love to those around us, then we are ignoring our responsibility as believers.

We should not only shine on stage with our anointing, ability, and talent, we must also shine to all the world around us.

Study Scriptures

- Psalm 147:1

- Isaiah 40:31
- Psalm 119:105
- Ephesians 6:13
- Deuteronomy 23:9
- Isaiah 1:18
- 1 Corinthians 2:16
- Ephesians 5:1-2
- 2 Corinthians 5:5-9
- Job 23:12

CHAPTER 11 TAKEAWAY KEY: Clipped Wings

You are called to great things, so don't let the enemy clip your wings and settle for second best. Don't give in to his lies that you are not good enough! Don't give into the lie that it's all about how many albums you sell and your marketing strategy. Always remember first and foremost it's all about your relationship with God. So if all God calls you to do is to pray and worship in your prayer closet, then that is exactly what you must do.

Your worship from your prayer closet is fueling the revival in your city. Jesus did this on a daily basis. In the morning He sought the Lord, and in the evening He sought the Lord. His relationship with God was first and foremost.

Only after Jesus was full of God could He minister to the people. If Jesus did life like this, then we must do the same. This is the way Jesus shined and so we must shine in the same way. This is the power of the secret place. We must find it and live in that place. That place is our source of life. The only way you can shine as a worship leader or as a believer is if you continually spend time in that place in God. That is the only way you will truly shine.

Don't give in to the lie that if all you do is serve in the local church you are not doing anything for the Kingdom. Guest ministers come and go, but you stay to keep the church strong and build the Kingdom.

Study Scriptures

- John 4:24
- James 5:16
- 2 Corinthians 4:12
- Matthew 5:14
- Mark 1:35
- Philippians 2:6-8
- John 14:10
- John 8:29
- John 14:9
- Psalm 91:1

CONCLUSION

WORSHIPPING WITHOUT LIMITS

In closing, I'd like to leave you with this final thought. Of course, *Worship Without Limits* was written to provide both spiritual and practical principles that will help churches move forward into transformational worship. However, it was also written to help build something else that is absolutely necessary for revival—unity in the Body of Christ.

Unity is the secret that causes a chain reaction of power that ultimately brings revival. We see this truth clearly presented in Scripture during the Day of Pentecost in Acts 2. The Bible says that the Holy Spirit came and baptized the disciples when they were all assembled in one accord. The outpouring of the Holy Spirit didn't happen until the disciples had come into unity.

Can you imagine what would have happened if the disciples had not been in unity? They would have missed God's appointed time of revival. Unity was critical to receiving God's power and to the advancement of the Kingdom.

I encourage you to be like the 120 disciples who waited together in unity for the power of the Holy Spirit. Pastor Paul Brady shared that it is his personal belief that there were more than 120 who initially gathered in the upper room, but only 120 waited patiently and in unity. I encourage you to be like those who waited for the promise...they were the ones who received God's power and turned the world upside down!

To be a vessel of God's power in our generation won't be easy. In fact, applying the principles I've taught in this book will be difficult. There will be days when you'll be excited to lead worship, and there will be days when it will seem like the greatest challenge of your life. Regardless of the testing or proving, be faithful. Don't give up. God will promote you in the end.

You may be tempted to quit when the pressure becomes the most intense, but don't stop obeying God right before your call becomes a reality. I encourage you to be like Jacob who wrestled with God. He wouldn't let go until he received his blessing (see Genesis 32:24-30). That blessing changed his life forever, just like God's blessing can revolutionize your own life. Stay strong, learn from your mistakes, and celebrate your victories.

Finally, I challenge you to be like a sponge that soaks in everything you need from the Lord. The more you soak in of God, the more He can squeeze out of you to bless others. God has anointed you for this time and this generation! Let that call and anointing propel you forward to your destiny. With God on your side, you can truly move in *worship without limits.*

TEN RULES OF WORSHIP

RULE 1 When leading people into worship, start off with a Scripture.

RULE 2 A worship leader is a leader of people, not just a singer.

RULE 3 Work together as a family.

RULE 4 Put others first in regard to melody and unity.

RULE 5 Maintain eye contact.

RULE 6 Learn new songs in five minutes and sing it comfortably or it's not a good fit.

RULE 7 Honor your pastor and those in leadership, above your personal opinion.

RULE 8 Must have a demonstration of your walk with God, on and off the stage.

RULE 9 Be a servant to all, no matter where you are serving.

RULE 10 Your power and success come from intimacy and time alone with God.

ABOUT THE AUTHOR

Philip Renner is an American missionary, author, worship leader, speaker, revivalist, and award-winning recording artist and songwriter. He leads Philip Renner Ministries and Renner Worship Music.

Philip was among the first national Russian language touring worship artists, teaching youth and church how to create their own original worship songs in their churches and city, with a foundation of fasting and prayer. Philip has played a significant role in bringing the sound of Heaven to many churches in Russia and neighboring countries.

The seeds of this worship movement began when he and his family answered the call to missions during the perilous time in the former USSR. They moved from Tulsa, Oklahoma, to Russia where they planted Moscow Good News Church, a currently thriving congregation of 4,000 in the heart of Moscow. Philip served for more than seven years as the youth pastor and worship leader under his father and pastor Rick Renner.

In 2013, Philip felt led to teach faith, missions, worship, prayer, and fasting, which resulted in hundreds of bookings, camps, conferences, festivals, and tours in Armenia, Belarus, Cypress, Georgia, Kazakhstan, Ukraine, Russia, the United Kingdom, and the United States. In the US, Philip has shared the stage with The Afters, Love & the Outcome, Misty Edwards, Rick Pino, and Travis Ryan.

Philip serves as worship leader in residence and speaker at Millennial Church in Tulsa, Oklahoma. He has appeared on TBN, LeSea TV *The Harvest Show,* Worship with Andy Chrisman, *Atlanta Live TV, Tulsa World,* TBN UK, Premier Radio UK, Cross Rhythms UK, and in *CCM Magazine.*

ABOUT THE AUTHOR

MINISTRY CONTACT INFORMATION

www.philiprenner.com

www.worshipwithoutlimitsbook.com

Instagram: philiprenner

Facebook: PhilipRennerMinistries

Twitter: PhilipRennerMin

LinkedIn: Philip Renner

General Inquiries: Info@philiprenner.com

Worship and Speaking Events: Jeff@onefive3management.com